THE
REALITY
OF
ANGELS

THE REALITY OF ANGELS

BY
LESTER SUMRALL

THOMAS NELSON PUBLISHERS
Nashville • Camden • New York

Copyright © 1982 by Lester Sumrall Evangelistic Association, Inc.

Published in Nashville, Tennessee, by Thomas Nelson, Inc. and distributed in Canada by Lawson Falle, Ltd., Cambridge, Ontario.

Printed in the United States of America.

Library of Congress Cataloging in Publication Data

Sumrall, Lester Frank, 1913-
  The reality of angels.

1. Angels.   I. Title.
BT966.2.S94   1982   235′.3   82-14498
ISBN 0-8407-5811-1

CONTENTS

INTRODUCTION

Never before in history has there been so much interest in supernatural phenomena. Many newspapers, magazines, and radio and television programs carry occasional items dealing with the occult, astrology, spiritism, exorcism, UFO's, and extrasensory perception. The film industry has found those subjects to be sure box-office hits.

Because of much misinformation and blatant falsehood presented about those topics, however, Christians have tended to shy away from anything supernatural. In doing so, they have ignored a vital area that God wants us to know about—the reality and ministry of angels.

There is a tremendous and exciting world of angelic existence, a world God has been pleased to reveal to us in the Bible, the only accurate sourcebook of information we have or need. I have made an exhaustive study of the nearly three hundred references to angels in the pages of the Old and New Testaments. In this book I present the results in a way I pray will be a rich blessing to you. May your spiritual eyes be opened wider by reading it.

THE
REALITY
OF
ANGELS

1
THE REALITY
OF
ANGELS

One morning during the Great Depression, while my father was away at work, someone knocked on the back door of our home. I opened it and saw a cleanly dressed individual standing there.

"I'm not a beggar," he said, "but I am hungry. Will you feed me?"

"Yes," replied my mother as she came to the door. "Come in."

While the meal was being prepared, the stranger sat at our table and talked about the wonderful truths in the Bible. He asked God's blessing on the food before he began to eat and after he had finished. Then he arose, looked at us for a few seconds, and walked out the door, closing it behind him.

My mother was the first to speak after he left. "Children, I have a very strange feeling about that visitor," she said.

Quickly, she opened the door and we all went out, but the stranger was nowhere to be seen. We looked into the street and all around the house. We searched fast; we searched diligently. But we could not find him.

As I think now about that incident from my boyhood years, I recall the words of Hebrews 13:2: "Be not forgetful to entertain strangers: for thereby some have entertained angels unawares."

Could that have been an angelic visitor to our home? I can't be sure, of course, but I do know that the Bible establishes beyond all doubt the reality of angels.

When we examine the Old Testament, for example, we find that angels are mentioned 108 times. Angels intervened in the lives of the patriarchs Abraham and Jacob, as the Book of Genesis indicates (see chaps. 18,19,28,32). Moses also knew the ministry of angels in his life, both in his call to return to Egypt (see Ex. 3:2) and during the wilderness wanderings (see Ex. 14:19). In all, the word *angel* or *angels* appears in the books of the Law, the writings of Moses, a total of 32 times.

Turn to the books of history and read of angelic activity in Joshua, Judges, 1 and 2 Samuel, 2 Kings, and in 1 and 2 Chronicles. Some 37 references to the work and ministry of angels relate to the development of the kingdom of Israel.

Those who wrote the books of poetry continued to unfold the existence of angels. The oldest book of the Bible, Job, speaks of angels (e.g.,

4:18). Frequently the Psalms describe angels as protecting and delivering God's people from all kinds of danger (see, e.g., 34:7; 91:11). With the exception of Jeremiah, all the major prophets alluded to the ministry of angels. The writer Daniel gave us the names of two angels, Gabriel (see Dan. 9:20-27) and Michael (see Dan. 10:13). Of the minor prophets, Hosea and Zechariah speak of angels.

The Old Testament writers did not feel it necessary to offer formal proof of angels or argue for their reality. Instead, the angels are assumed to exist, just as God is assumed to exist.

The Old Testament alone would be sufficient to establish the fact of angels, but the New Testament continues to enlarge our knowledge of angelic beings. In fact, although the New Testament is far shorter than the Old, angels arc mentioned there even more often—a total of 165 times. The gospels are filled with references to them, and six times in the Book of Acts, angels ministered to the Lord's people (e.g., 5:18-20).

The writer of half the epistles, Paul, spoke of angels in many of the books that bear his name. James and Peter spoke of them in their letters, too.

The last division of the New Testament, the Revelation, refers to angels no fewer than 65 times. (Later, we shall consider those references in detail.)

Surely, all these mentions of the reality and ministry of angels are convincing, but there is also the testimony of the Lord Jesus Christ. It was He, of course, who created angels in the beginning, so it comes as no surprise that He believed in and taught the existence of angels. (see, e.g., Matt. 13:39-41).

Angels are real. We know that with absolute certainty from the Bible and from the Son of God.

What are angels? Who are angels? Let's define them this way: Angels are created, spirit beings. We know angels are created from reading Psalm 148:2,5: "Praise ye him, all his angels: praise ye him, all his hosts. ... Let them praise the name of the LORD: for he commanded, and they were created." We know angels are spirit beings because of passages like Hebrews 1:14: "Are they not all ministering spirits, sent forth to minister for them who shall be heirs of salvation?"

Another helpful definition of angels comes through the Greek and Hebrew words for them. *Angel* literally means "messenger." Angels are the heavenly messengers of God, often delivering His messages to men and women.

Now that we have looked at the reality of angels and have defined their name, let me give you a general overview of angels by making a number of "angels are" statements.

No Dying, No Death

First, *angels are immortal.* Some Sadducees once came to Jesus, trying to trap Him on the subject of the resurrection, an idea which they rejected. They wanted to know, so they said, about the case of a woman who had in succession seven husbands. Whose wife would she be in the resurrection (see Luke 20:27-33)?

Jesus replied that, in heaven, people neither marry nor are given in marriage. Then He added, "Neither can they die any more: for they are equal unto the angels" (Luke 20:36).

Angels never get sick, never go to the hospital, never die. You'll never read an obituary for an angel. You'll never go to an angel's funeral. God created angels to live forever.

Outranking Man

Angels are of a high order. Do you remember from your school days how you learned to rank things in their proper order? A comes before B. One comes before two. Life comes in order: human, animal, plant. You can cite many examples.

Where do angels rank in the created order of God? The Bible tells us that angels constitute a higher form than man. Psalm 8:5 declares, "For thou hast made him [man] a little lower than the angels, and hast crowned him with glory and honor." And in 2 Peter 2:11 we read that angels are greater in power and might than human beings.

Even so, angels rank far below God Himself. Lucifer, you will remember, was one of the angels who aspired to rise above God, as Isaiah 14 relates, but he failed. He didn't have that power.

Sometimes when a child learns about angels, he may say, "I'd like to be one!" No, God has something far better for those who believe in Jesus Christ. In fact, one day, in our exalted, heavenly state, we shall judge the angels (see 1 Cor. 6:3).

Keen-minded

Angels are intelligent. Recently a young man was interviewed on television and was said to have an I.Q. of 206. That's simply amazing. But he wouldn't fare too well in a one-to-one confrontation with an angel. Angels have great intelligence. In 2 Samuel 14:20 we read about being wise "according to the wisdom of an angel of God, to know all things that are in the earth."

There are some things, of course, that angels don't know, such as the hour of our Lord's return from heaven (see Matt. 24:36). But angels want to know all they can about what God is doing. For example, they are trying to understand God's great plan of salvation for mankind (1

Pet. 1:12). I've never heard the expression "smart as an angel," but perhaps we should coin it.

No Sin, No Stain

Angels are holy. When we consider that angels constantly dwell in the presence of God, we can well understand that they, too, must be holy. Mark 8:38 speaks specifically of angels as being holy. That's the way He created them.

Have you ever seen drawings of angels done by various artists? Always they are pictured as being clothed in white, representing their purity as revealed in Scripture.

Count Them if You Can

Angels are innumerable. Men and women have often wondered how many angels there are. We are told that during the Middle Ages some people used to stand around debating how many angels could stand on the head of a pin. That would be nothing but vain speculation, of course, but still our minds wonder how many angels God created.

Once again, Scripture gives us a little information. Hebrews 12:22 speaks of those who "are come unto mount Zion, and unto the city of the living God, the heavenly Jerusalem, and to an innumerable company of angels." The word *innumerable* means one thing: You cannot count them. The group is so vast that numbers cannot be assigned.

The Book of Job gives us the same idea in this reference to God's angelic armies: "Is there any number of his armies?" (25:3).

The shepherds were given an incredible view of the angelic multitudes on the night our Savior was born. "And suddenly there was with the angel a multitude of the heavenly host praising God, and saying, Glory to God in the highest, and on earth peace, good will toward men" (Luke 2:13,14). How many angels came to take part in that announcement and call to worship, we do not know. Perhaps the entire sky as far as the shepherds could see was filled with the heavenly messengers. What a sight!

No Need for Workouts

Angels are strong. Second Thessalonians 1:7 tells us of a coming day "when the Lord Jesus shall be revealed from heaven with his mighty angels." Why do they need to be strong? Because they will perform all the things for God that need doing on the face of this earth. Perhaps Revelation 18:1 gives us one good example: "And after these things I saw another angel come down from heaven, having great power; and the earth was lightened with his glory." Imagine that angel of superhuman strength lighting up the darkness with his appearance.

Consider also Psalm 103:20, which teaches that angels "excel in strength." Outside the Godhead, there is no order of creation any stronger. Angels are able to act effectively, with power, because they were given that ability by God.

Out of Sight

Angels are invisible. Although men and women have seen angels many times, as recorded in the Bible, we must remember that angels are spirits and only take on forms visible to human beings on relatively rare occasions, when God has them do so for some specific reason. We see an example of how they do God's work even when invisible to man in Numbers 22:22-31.

Not Made for Marriage

Angels do not marry. We do not know why the Lord Jesus chose to tell us this, but in Matthew's gospel we are informed that angels do not marry (see 22:30). We are not told anywhere in Scripture whether there are even female angels, and it would be pointless to speculate about the matter. What we do know, simply, is that angels do not participate in the institution of marriage.

That fact does tell us a little about angelic service to God, however, especially in light of the apostle Paul's advice to Christians in 1 Corinthians 7. In that chapter, he explained that it is good, if one feels so led, to remain unmarried in order to devote full attention to serving and pleasing God (see vv. 32-34). The married person must please his spouse as well as God, but the single person can concentrate exclusively on the Lord.

Therefore, since angels do not marry, they are free to give their full devotion to God. There are no distractions, no earthly companions whose pleasure they might seek above the Lord's. They can be single-minded in going about the purposes for which God created them.

Sing for Joy

Angels are joyful. Could angels possibly have long faces or be depressed? I think not because of Luke 15:10: "Likewise, I say unto you, there is joy in the presence of the angels of God over one sinner that repenteth." In this world there is somebody being saved every moment of the day. Somebody is finding God, somewhere. Thus, what a good time angels must have! They are constantly filled with joy because of sinners coming to know Jesus as their personal Savior. When we consider that angels dwell in heaven with God and serve Him in holiness, they have great cause, indeed, for joy.

No, Don't Do It

When we stop to consider how wonderful the angels are, we may feel that we ought to make a little statue and bow down to worship them. In a sense, that must have been the way the apostle John felt when he was given all the tremendous insights he recorded in the Book of the Revelation. Read what he wrote:

> And I John saw these things, and heard them. And when I had heard and seen, I fell down to worship before the feet of the angel which showed me these things. Then saith he unto me, See thou do it not: for I am thy fellow servant, and of thy brethren the prophets, and of them which keep the sayings of this book: worship God (Rev. 22:8,9).

So not only does the Bible say we must not worship angels, but it also says that angels do not want to be worshiped.

The apostle Paul also spoke to the matter of angel worship: "Let no man beguile you of your reward in a voluntary humility and worshiping of angels, intruding into those things which he hath not seen" (Col. 2:18). So if someone says to you, in effect, "We ought to worship angels," don't listen to him. He's wrong. His teaching is contrary to God's Word.

This has been a brief introduction to the great theme of angels. We've looked at just a few of the characteristics angels possess. Is this an important study? It is, indeed, particularly in the time in which we live. It is my earnest belief that in these last days we are going to see more angels, see more of their work and power, than at any other time since that recorded in Revelation. There are going to be tremendous things happening in the very near future, and we don't want through unbelief or unconcern to be blinded to or to miss what God is doing in our time.

2
CATEGORIES OF ANGELS— THEIR NAMES AND RANKS

Whether you ever served in the armed forces or not, I'm sure you are acquainted with how the military ranks its enlisted men and officers. In the army, for example, we have generals at the top and then down through colonels, majors, captains, and lieutenants. And enlisted men also may be identified by different ranks and responsibilities.

Do you know that God also ranks angels? Our Lord even used a military term once in connection with angels. When Jesus was about to be taken in the Garden of Gethsemane, Peter took out a sword and tried to protect the One he had come to love and serve. Jesus said, "Thinkest thou that I cannot now pray to my Father, and he shall presently give me more than twelve legions of angels?" (Matt. 26:53). The word *legion* was a Roman military designation referring to about six thousand soldiers.

The Heavenly Host

In a general sense, probably the largest

group of angels is what we might call the "ordinary" angels. Most of the time when angels are mentioned in the Bible, it is these otherwise unidentified angels who are being referred to. To speak of ordinary angels seems a contradiction in terms, however, for how could these extraordinary, created beings be considered just something routine? Yet in one sense, this designation is proper when we contrast them with the several special classes, or orders, of angels that the Bible mentions.

Cherubim

Judging from various Scripture references, I believe the cherubim rank at the very top of God's angelic creation, both in power and in beauty. They are, in fact, the first of the angelic order to appear in the Bible, right after Adam's and Eve's fall from grace. Genesis 3 records the events in the Garden of Eden. Having violated God's command not to partake of the tree of the knowledge of good and evil, it would have been possible for Adam and Eve to reach out their hands and "take also of the tree of life, and eat, and live for ever" (v. 22). So they had to be expelled from their earthly paradise. "Therefore the Lord God sent him forth from the garden of Eden, to till the ground from whence he was taken" (v. 23).

But what would have prevented Adam from

returning to the garden to disobey God once more? The next verse gives the answer: "He [God] placed at the east of the garden of Eden cherubim, and a flaming sword which turned every way, to keep the way of the tree of life" (v. 24).

What a terrible thing it would have been if Adam had eaten of the Tree of Life and so have been forever confirmed in his fallen state! To prevent that, God sent a contingent of glorious and trusted cherubim to guard access to the tree. What Adam's reaction was to seeing for the first time in human history those glorious cherubim, we are not told. Awe, fright, wonder — perhaps Adam experienced all those emotions as the truth struck home that his act of sin had severed him from the fellowship and presence of a holy God.

Strangely enough, the next appearance of the cherubim in the Bible concerns regaining what was lost. In Exodus 25, Moses was given explicit and detailed instructions on how to make various articles of furniture that would be used in the tabernacle. The first described was the ark of the covenant and the mercy seat, where God promised to meet and commune with Moses.

What did God wish placed on top of, or over, the mercy seat? He chose representations of the cherubim, in gold. Read the fascinating description God gave Moses:

And thou shalt make two cherubim of gold, of beaten work shalt thou make them, in the two ends of the mercy seat. And make one cherub on the one end, and the other cherub on the other end: even of the mercy seat shall ye make the cherubim on the two ends thereof. And the cherubim shall stretch forth their wings on high, covering the mercy seat with their wings, and their faces shall look one to another; toward the mercy seat shall the faces of the cherubim be (Ex. 25:18-20).

What a great sight that must have been—the cherubim associated with the very presence of God.

From those two references in Scripture, it appears as though the cherubim's major responsibility may be to declare the sinfulness of man and protect the presence of God from sinful men. No doubt Adam never forgot the sight of the cherubim as he longed to return to the Garden of Eden, but they reminded him that he had transgressed the commandment of God. Once a year, the high priest of Israel would be permitted into the Holy of Holies; there he could look upon the mercy seat. I'm sure he must have felt on each occasion, "I don't belong here in the holy presence of God, for I am a sinner."

Seraphim

Another group of angels specifically identified are the seraphim. In the Hebrew language, *seraphim* means "burning ones." Burning how? Why? I believe it refers to their burning devotion toward God from hearts that are on fire to serve Him.

Isaiah 6 tells us of the seraphim. Isaiah recorded his glorious vision in these words:

> I saw also the Lord sitting upon a throne, high and lifted up, and his train filled the temple. Above it stood the seraphim: each one had six wings; with twain he covered his face, and with twain he covered his feet, and with twain he did fly (vv. 1,2).

What were the seraphim doing? "And one cried unto another, and said, Holy, holy, holy, is the LORD of hosts: the whole earth is full of his glory" (v. 3).

The prophet recognized at once that he had no right to be in the holy presence of God, and he confessed as much. So one of the seraphim took a burning coal from the altar and touched Isaiah's lips to cleanse his iniquity and purge his sin (vv. 5-7).

So, seraphim have wings. They proclaim the holiness of God. They indicate to men their need to be cleansed from sin.

Living Creatures

A third special group of angels is called, in the King James version, "the four beasts," but a better translation would be "the four living creatures." These angels, like the seraphim, have six wings. Revelation 4:8 declares, "And the four beasts [living creatures] had each of them six wings about him; and they were full of eyes within: and they rest not day and night, saying, Holy, holy, holy, Lord God Almighty, which was, and is, and is to come."

Their special ministry, then, is to worship God and give Him glory throughout all time and eternity. We read of them again in Revelation 5, 7, and 19. In each instance they are depicted in an attitude of worship and praise. In Revelation 15, however, they participate in the pouring out of the wrath of God on unrepentant men.

It may be that the living creatures have other duties God has not revealed to us. But the brief insights given are intended, I believe, to draw us up short to a realization that God is holy and will not let sin go unpunished.

Michael

Another angelic rank, archangel, is held by only one angel in the biblical record. The word *arch* means "chief," so this angel is the most prominent of all the holy angels.

The archangel's name is Michael. That name asks a question: "Who is like God?" Probably many parents, both Jews and Gentiles, who call their boys Michael have no idea what the name conveys. That's unfortunate. It would be great if the minds and hearts of people were directed to God each time they heard the name. Often in Scripture, as we shall see, men who received angelic visitations wanted to worship the creation rather than the Creator. So how appropriate it is that the name of Michael, the archangel, invites us to direct our attention to almighty God.

The prophet Daniel introduces us to Michael. It seems that he had been praying, and God had dispatched an answer by the hand of a messenger who was hindered on his journey until, he testified, "Michael, one of the chief princes, came to help me" (Dan. 10:13). So Michael had to fight for the free passage of God's Word.

It might be appropriate to give Michael the title of general, for each time we see him, it is in connection with some type of spiritual struggle. In his role as a fighter, Michael has a particular responsibility to Israel. In Daniel 10:21 and 12:1, he is said to be the prince of that nation. As we read ancient and modern history, I believe we see the hand of Michael defending Israel. As you know, that little nation has fought four wars with its Arab neighbors since gaining statehood in 1948. The Arabs have often expressed their determination to drive Israel into the sea, but they have never been able to accomplish that feat. Could it be because Michael is on the side of Israel, influencing strategy and insuring victory? I think that may well be the case.

In addition to the Old Testament references, we also find Michael mentioned in the New Testament. In the little Book of Jude, the ninth verse specifically calls Michael an archangel and recounts his battle with Lucifer over the body of Moses. With the Lord's help, Michael won.

That wasn't the only conflict between Michael and Lucifer, for John tells us in the Book of Revelation,

> And there was war in heaven: Michael and his angels fought against the dragon; and the dragon fought and his angels. And prevailed not; neither was their place found any more in heaven. And the great dragon was cast out, that old serpent, called the Devil, and Satan, which deceiveth the whole world: he was cast out into the earth, and his angels were cast out with him (12:7-9).

Here we see Michael serving as commanding officer of a large group of angels. Evidently, Michael is the chief warrior of God.

Gabriel

The only other angel whose name is given in Scripture (besides Lucifer) is Gabriel. The meaning of *Gabriel* is "mighty one of God." He lives up to his name, for he does, indeed, do mighty things. Rather than being a fighter like Michael, Gabriel serves God more as a messenger. He appears several times in the Book of Daniel to give important revelations concerning future events, especially relating to God's kingdom. After one of Daniel's visions, for example, the prophet wondered about its meaning. Then suddenly, "There stood before me as the appearance of a man. And I heard a man's voice between the banks of Ulai, which called, and said, Gabriel, make this man to understand the vision" (Dan. 8:15,16). Gabriel did. We have something similar in Daniel 9, where, following Daniel's prayer of confession of sin on behalf of his people, Gabriel again came to him, "being caused to fly swiftly" (v. 21).

Thus, in the Old Testament, we see Gabriel's ministry in connection with the kingdom. In the New Testament, he is concerned with the King. In the first instance, Zacharias was waiting before the Lord in the Temple. Suddenly, "there appeared unto him an angel of the Lord standing on the right side of the altar of incense" (Luke 1:11). Gabriel identified himself to Zacharias: "I am Gabriel, that stand in the presence of God; and am sent to speak unto thee, and to show thee these glad tidings" (Luke 1:19). That good news concerned the coming birth of John the Baptist, who would be the forerunner of the Lord Jesus, ruler of Israel and the world.

It was this same Gabriel whom God sent one

day to the city of Nazareth "to a virgin espoused to a man whose name was Joseph, of the house of David; and the virgin's name was Mary" (Luke 1:27). What a great announcement Gabriel had to give to that young lady: "Thou shalt conceive in thy womb, and bring forth a son, and shalt call his name JESUS. He shall be great, and shall be called the Son of the Highest: and the Lord God shall give unto him the throne of his father David" (vv. 31,32).

Gabriel, then, is the one who bore the message of God concerning the coming kingdom and the King. God gave this specific angel that tremendous privilege and responsibility.

Lucifer

We learn the original name of the angel Satan in Isaiah 14:12. That verse not only names him but also tells us something vital about him: "How art thou fallen from heaven, O Lucifer, son of the morning! how art thou cut down to the ground, which didst weaken the nations!" Once, Lucifer was up there with God. But not any longer. Why? He was cast down because of his pride and ambition:

> For thou hast said in thine heart, I will ascend into heaven, I will exalt my throne above the stars of God; I will sit also upon the mount of the congregation, in the sides of the north: I will ascend above the heights of the clouds; I will be like the most High" (Is. 14:13,14).

Because of his own ego, and because of his promotion of himself, Lucifer lost his lofty position in heaven. He fell from the Father's divine grace.

So where does he operate now? He is right here on earth. Two different times our Lord described Lucifer as being the prince of this world (see John 12:31; 16:11). This earth on which we live is under his authority.

While the angels Michael and Gabriel have only single names, so far as we know, Lucifer has many that indicate facets of his evil character. Many people are better acquainted with two of his other names, Satan and the devil. Jesus also called him the evil one (see John 17:15). The Book of Revelation assigns him a virtual dictionary of names, including the old serpent, the great dragon, the destroyer, the accuser, and the deceiver. I often think of Lucifer by another of his names, that of tempter, for it was he who came to tempt Jesus during his stay in the wilderness (see Matt. 4:1,3).

We will look more closely at Satan and his demons in Chapter 8.

Holy Ones and Watchers

There are various minor categories of angels mentioned in the Bible, such as holy ones and watchers. Babylonian King Nebuchadnezzar reported, "I saw in the visions of my head upon my bed, and behold, a watcher and a holy one came down from heaven" (Dan. 4:13). They announced judgment "by the decree of the watchers, and the demand by the word of the holy ones" (4:17). Then, "the king saw a watcher and a holy one coming down from heaven" (4:23).

Could these watchers and holy ones still be at work today? It's an interesting thought. Nebuchadnezzar was overthrown because of his sin. From time to time, we read of contemporary rulers being overthrown as well. It may be that these angels continue to decree the downfall of sinful nations.

Godly Thrones, Dominions, Principalities, Powers

There are two passages from the writings of the apostle Paul that seem very similar at first glance. Let me show you a difference. In Colossians 1:15,16, we read these words:

[Jesus] is the image of the invisible God, the first-born of every creature: for by him were all things created, that are in heaven, and that are in earth, visible and invisible, whether they be thrones, or dominions, or principalities, or powers: all things were created by him and for him.

Those classifications seem to refer to godly powers of angelic orders. We have very little information about them other than their names.

In the Book of Ephesians, Paul used similar words, but this time with a different reference. We are told to

> put on the whole armor of God, that ye may be able to stand against the wiles of the devil. For we wrestle not against flesh and blood, but against principalities, against powers, against the rulers of the darkness of this world, against spiritual wickedness in high places (6:11,12).

These are obviously evil angelic hosts.

God is in control of those wicked forces and even uses them for His purposes. For example, He used them to afflict the Egyptians prior to the Exodus: "He cast upon them the fierceness of his anger, wrath, and indignation, and trouble, by sending evil angels among them" (Ps. 78:49).

Those are some of the angelic ranks. God in His wisdom has not given us as much information about the names of angelic orders as we might like. He has simply lifted the curtain of heaven a bit so that we might catch a glimpse of those spiritual beings in their activity on behalf of God and man.

3
WHAT ANGELS DO

Does the company you work for have a job description for your position? Most firms do that sort of thing. The personnel office of almost every large concern, and many smaller ones as well, draws up a list of tasks for which each employee is responsible. It may give the qualifications for each job, too, and indicate the persons to whom employees must report.

That's a good approach. That way, there is no misunderstanding on the part of the boss or the worker about what is expected. Everything is open and on the table.

In a very real sense, the Bible gives us a job description for angels. Yes, God has been pleased both by way of deliberate teaching and by way of example to show us at least some of what His marvelous angelic creation does. Not all angels do the same things, of course, for the Lord has made various assignments.

God's angels are active. In this chapter, I'd like to show you some of the important things angels do. Let's take as our general reference point an outstanding verse from the Bible: "For he shall give his angels charge over thee, to keep thee in all thy ways" (Ps. 91:11). This affirms that it is God who gives angels their responsibilities and that many of their activities are on our behalf.

Worship First

Before angels do anything for human beings, they first continue their ministry to God in praise and worship. Often my mind and heart return to that scene foretold in Revelation 7:11: "And all the angels stood round about the throne, and about the elders and the four beasts, and fell before the throne on their faces, and worshiped God."

The Bible gives us several such pictures of angels worshiping God. We have already seen the seraphim proclaiming God to be "holy, holy, holy" in Isaiah 6:3. And in Revelation 5:11,12 we read: "And I beheld, and I heard the voice of many angels round about the throne and the beasts and the elders ... saying with a loud voice, Worthy is the Lamb that was slain to receive power, and riches, and wisdom, and strength, and honor, and glory, and blessing."

The angels provide a good pattern for us to follow. How often do we rush off to serve God or others, perhaps in some good and necessary way, and neglect to first worship God and adore

Him. Of course we should give God and others our every effort in service. But before that, we need to spend time in His presence, getting our hearts tuned up.

Go This Way

Certainly it must have happened to you—getting lost as you searched for some unfamiliar address. Perhaps you became completely disoriented. That can be frightening. So you pull into a service station, if one is available and open, and ask for directions. Maybe you buy a map. Then how comforting it can be to get your bearings and head out confidently for your destination.

The need for clear direction in spiritual matters is very important. One great thing angels occasionally do is to direct believers.

Three men who were once very glad about the reality of angelic direction were Abraham, a servant, and a son. Abraham's son Isaac was unmarried, and Abraham wanted to find a wife for him. So the patriarch sent off the eldest of his servants on the extremely important mission of finding a wife for Isaac among his relatives in the land from which God had originally called him (see Gen. 24).

Perhaps the servant was fearful that he might make the wrong choice. Abraham said something to him that was reassuring: "He [God] shall send his angel before thee, and thou shalt take a wife unto my son from thence" (Gen. 24:7).

That's exactly what took place. An angel led the servant directly to the beautiful, young Rebekah, and she readily agreed to leave her home and people to become the bride of Isaac.

For another example of angelic direction, jump ahead several hundred years in the history of God's people to the time of the judges. Under great oppression, the Israelites cried out to the Lord, and He determined to send them deliverance through the man Gideon. "And the angel of the LORD appeared unto him, and said unto him, The LORD is with thee, thou mighty man of valor" (Judg. 6:12). Then this angel went on to tell Gideon just how he was to go about the job of freeing God's people from their enemies. Gideon didn't have to guess what he was to do or how he was to do it. The Lord gave specific direction through His angel.

The New Testament gives us other fine examples of angelic leadership. It happened to Philip, one of the original seven deacons. The Lord wanted to direct him to a special evangelistic task. But how would that direction be given? "And the angel of the Lord spake unto Philip, saying, Arise, and go toward the south unto the way that goeth down from Jerusalem unto Gaza, which is desert" (Acts 8:26). Philip obeyed at once, and from that point on, the Holy Spirit guided him.

The man Cornelius needed to know about the salvation that could be found only in the Lord Jesus Christ. So he was directed by an angel to send for Peter (see Acts 10:3-5).

Do angels perform this same service today, this ministry of providing direction for God's people? I'm confident they do, though, of course, it can't be proved one way or the other. I have often felt when I have gone to do something or to reach somebody that God's angel directed me and had gone on before. Isn't that beautiful?

You're Safe!

Angels also protect believers. We have many instances of such protection recorded in the Bible. The apostle Paul could tell you about that. Remember the time his ship was caught in a terrible storm as he went to Rome? It seemed certain that the vessel would be lost and all on board would drown. The sailors did everything they possibly could, but they recognized they were facing death (see Acts 27:14-20).

Then Paul went to them and told them to be of good cheer. How could he say that? How did he know? What inside information did he have? He told them:

> There shall be no loss of any man's life among you, but of the ship. For there stood by me this

night the angel of God, whose I am, and whom
I serve, saying, Fear not, Paul; thou must be
brought before Caesar: and, lo, God hath given
thee all them that sail with thee (Acts
27:22-24).

With that angelic assurance of protection, no
wonder Paul could encourage them to cheer up.

God's Word gives us other examples of how
angels protect His people. An angel shut the
mouths of lions as Daniel spent the night in
their den (see Dan. 6:16-23). Three young Hebrew men—Shadrach, Meshach, and Abed-
nego—seemed certain to burn to death after
being cast into the furnace heated seven times
hotter than it ought to have been. God's angel
kept them from harm (see Dan. 3:1-28).

Think back on your life, my friend. Perhaps
you were spared some horrible accident that
could have seriously injured you or even killed
you. You came through without a scratch. Could
an angel have been on duty to save you in your
moment of peril? Don't be surprised to learn
some day in heaven that that is what took place.

Information, Please

One of the main ministries of angels to human beings is to convey information from God
to us. We have already looked at a few cases in
which angels served as God's messengers:

when angels spoke to the pagan King Nebu-chadnezzar in a dream, and when Gabriel prophesied the births of John the Baptist and the Lord Jesus.

There have been many times when men have needed messages from God and angels have delivered them. Consider, for example, the enormous burden that rested on the shoulders of Moses as he undertook the leadership of God's people. They needed commandments, for one thing, so that they would know how to live lives pleasing to God. Angels had some part in that—exactly what we don't know—for we read that the nation Israel "received the law by the disposition of angels" (Acts 7:53).

Prophets such as Daniel and Zechariah were given visions that they could not interpret by their own wisdom. So God used angels to explain (see Dan. 7:15-27; 8:13-26; Zech. 4:1; 5:5; 6:5).

In the Christmas story we all know so well, the shepherds were informed by angels of the time and place of the birth of God's Son (see Luke 2:8-14). Later, an angel warned Joseph to flee with Mary and the infant Jesus to Egypt because Herod wanted to kill Jesus (see Matt. 2:13).

An angel also had the joyous responsibility of announcing Jesus' resurrection to the women who came to His tomb on the first Easter morning (see Matt. 28:5-7). Imagine how those women felt as they received this news from such a marvelous being (see 28:3)!

As God has relayed information through angels in these and many other cases in the past, so also He could provide information to you at some time of special need in the future. We don't know, of course, when God will choose to use that extraordinary means of communication, and we can find principles in the Bible to give general guidance to every decision and action. God still can supply information through angels, and He could speak to you that way some day.

"Coming for to Carry Me Home"

In recent years, popular books by medical doctors and psychologists have attempted to establish the fact of life after death. Often they include the case histories of people who have died, at least from a clinical standpoint. Those individuals try to tell us what it is like to leave their bodies behind on hospital beds and venture into the unknown. Yet, I find such mystic accounts unsatisfying and sometimes contradictory.

How much better it is to turn to the authoritative Word of God. In Luke 16, our Lord Himself related what happened at the deaths of a rich man and Lazarus, a beggar. "And it came to pass, that the beggar died, and was carried by the angels into Abraham's bosom" (v. 22). I love that. When my dear mother died, I believe that she, too, was escorted right into the very presence of God and the saints who went before her by an angel.

It is difficult and even dangerous to make a general statement from just one passage of Scripture, but I like to think that all believers who die do receive that angelic service. If that's true, you, too, when you leave this earth in death — should the Lord delay His return — won't have to grope to find your way. You won't have to wonder who is going to introduce you. An angel will take care of those things for you. With great joy he will take your soul from here to there.

Angels Bring Judgment

We have examples in the Bible of times in which God used and will use angels to send judgment. One of these took place during the kingship of David, and it's frightening. "And Satan stood up against Israel, and provoked David to number Israel" (1 Chr. 21:1). Apparently, David wanted to find out just how strong he was militarily, and that showed a lack of trust in God. So God had to send terrible punishment.

> The LORD sent pestilence upon Israel: and there fell of Israel seventy thousand men. And God sent an angel unto Jerusalem to destroy it:

and as he was destroying, the LORD beheld, and he repented him of the evil, and said to the angel that destroyed, It is enough, stay now thine hand (1 Chr. 21:14,15).

Even earlier in Israel's history, God used an angel to execute judgment on Egypt for the Pharaoh's hardness of heart in refusing to allow Israel to leave. As the culmination of the various plagues God had brought on Egypt, He sent an angel of death, "the destroyer" (Ex. 12:23), to kill all the first-born in every Egyptian household.

And it came to pass, that at midnight the LORD smote all the first-born in the land of Egypt, from the first-born of Pharaoh that sat on his throne unto the first-born of the captive that was in the dungeon; and all the first-born of cattle. And Pharaoh rose up in the night, he, and all his servants, and all the Egyptians; and there was a great cry in Egypt; for there was not a house where there was not one dead (Ex. 12:29,30).

In the New Testament, we have the account of King Herod's giving a speech that caused his audience to declare him a god, a declaration he did nothing to discourage (see Acts 12:21,22). In response to that blasphemy, "immediately the angel of the Lord smote him, because he gave not God the glory: and he was eaten of worms, and gave up the ghost" (Acts 12:23).

We also know that angels will be instruments of God's judgment on sinful humanity in the end times. In His parable of the wheat and tares in Matthew 13, Jesus said, "The field is the world; the good seed are the children of the kingdom; but the tares are the children of the wicked one; the enemy that sowed them is the devil; the harvest is the end of the world; and the reapers are the angels" (vv. 38,39).

That time of the Great Tribulation will be the grimmest hour the world has ever known. Jesus continued, "The Son of man shall send forth his angels, and they shall gather out of his kingdom all things that offend, and them which do iniquity; and shall cast them into a furnace of fire: there shall be wailing and gnashing of teeth" (vv. 41,42).

There are also scenes of angels dispensing God's end-times judgments throughout the Book of the Revelation.

Helpers of the Great Physician?

We know God heals. Is it possible that angels are somehow involved in His work of healing? That suggestion comes to us from reading about a miracle of healing performed by our Lord Jesus. He restored a man who had been sick for thirty-eight years. And in that account, the Bible tells us that poor man had sought healing with many others at a pool called Bethesda.

> In these lay a great multitude of impotent folk, of blind, halt, withered, waiting for the moving of the water. For an angel went down at a certain season into the pool, and troubled the water: whosoever then first after the troubling of the water stepped in was made whole of whatsoever disease he had (John 5:3,4).

Providing Food and Water

As we read through the Bible, we see a number of instances in which God used angels to provide the physical necessities of food and drink when they were not normally available. The first of those is found in Genesis 21, which records the conclusion of the story of Hagar. Abraham had to send her and her son away, yet he loved her and the lad Ishmael. So he gave them bread and a bottle of water before they left to go out into the desert.

Soon, however, those provisions were depleted. Hagar was sure they were going to die. She and Ishmael cried out to God and wept.

> And God heard the voice of the lad; and the angel of God called to Hagar out of heaven, and said unto her, What aileth thee, Hagar? fear not; for God hath heard the voice of the lad where he is. . . . And God opened her eyes, and she saw a well of water; and she went, and filled

the bottle with water, and gave the lad drink
(Gen. 21:17,19).

What a touching story! What a gracious God!

There is a similar story in the life of Elijah.
Immediately after his well-known confrontation with and victory over the prophets of Baal,
his life was threatened by Jezebel. Elijah lost
all his courage and took off like a scared rabbit,
running for many miles. Finally he sat down
under a tree and gave up. "O Lord," he prayed,
"take away my life; for I am not better than my
fathers" (1 Kin. 19:4).

God's ministry for Elijah, however, was not
over. How would He intervene in this situation?
The following verses tell us: "An angel touched
him, and said unto him, Arise and eat. And he
looked, and, behold, there was a cake baked on
the coals, and a cruse of water at his head. And
he did eat and drink" (vv. 5,6). That was a private, personal miracle extended by God
through an angel to His servant Elijah, but God
wasn't finished. God repeated the provision,
and the prophet received so much strength and
encouragement that he was able to go on traveling another forty days and continue his needed
ministry (see vv. 7,8).

If God would reach down and supply the
needs of individuals like Hagar and Elijah, it
should not surprise us to learn in the New Testament that He did the same for His beloved

Son. After Jesus had fasted for forty days and nights, He was tempted by the devil. One of those temptations, you will recall, involved the turning of a stone into bread (see Matt. 4:3). Our Lord easily could have done it but that would have been using His power wrongfully to supply a personal need suggested by the tempter.

After the third temptation, the devil left Jesus, who was still hungry. What happened? "Angels came and ministered unto him" (Matt. 4:11). Although we are not told so specifically, it seems apparent that food and drink were provided, perhaps the same as that given to Elijah in his time of need.

Do angels minister to God's people in this manner in modern times? George Müller thought so. That great Englishman of the last century provided care for scores of orphans. Sometimes, he had nothing to place on the table before them, but somehow, unexpectedly, from some source, food would be provided and the children would not go hungry. Perhaps God used angels once again to give food and drink when human resources failed.

God's Warriors

God also uses angels as armies to fight for Him and His people. As we saw earlier when studying Michael the archangel, there was a war in heaven between Michael and his angels and Satan and his angels when Satan rebelled against God (see Rev. 12). The holy angels prevailed, and Satan and his angels were cast to the earth.

In 2 Kings 19, we see God sending an angel to fight for Israel in defense of Jerusalem. In verse 34, God promised to defend the city, and in verse 35 we read: "And it came to pass that night, that the angel of the LORD went out, and smote in the camp of the Assyrians a hundred fourscore and five thousand: and when they arose early in the morning, behold, they were all dead corpses."

Another good example of angels as warriors is given to us in 2 Kings 6. The king of Syria was waging war against Israel, but he could not capture the king of Israel, because the prophet Elisha was giving his king knowledge from God of the Syrians' plans. When the king of Syria was told that, he ascertained that Elisha was in Dothan and sent a large group of his soldiers and chariots there to capture Elisha.

Those soldiers arrived at night and encircled the city. "And when the servant of the man of God was risen early, and gone forth, behold, a host compassed the city both with horses and chariots. And his servant said unto him, Alas, my master! how shall we do?" (2 Kin. 6:15).

Obviously, the servant thought he and Elisha were in a lot of trouble. We can well understand how frightened he must have been as he looked out over the enemy.

But Elisha knew that God was on his side and that awesome angelic forces were available to fight for him if need be. So he said, "Fear not: for they that be with us are more than they that be with them" (6:16). Because he wanted the servant to be as confident of that as he was, "Elisha prayed, and said, LORD, I pray thee, open his eyes, that he may see. And the LORD opened the eyes of the young man; and he saw: and, behold, the mountain was full of horses and chariots of fire round about Elisha" (6:17).

That fiery army, invisible to the Syrians, was made up of angelic powers sent by God.

Heavenly Encouragement

We all need encouragement on occasion, and sometimes when God's servants have been in special need, He has sent angels to provide it.

In Daniel 9:21, the angel Gabriel came to Daniel to give him an encouraging touch. Gabriel then told him a prophecy.

As we saw earlier, when Paul was on his way to Rome, the boat he was in got caught in a severe storm that threatened the lives of everyone aboard. But an angel came to Paul at night and encouraged him with God's promise that everyone would be saved (see Acts 27:23,24).

Our Lord Himself probably received angelic encouragement many times during His life on earth. The night of His greatest need was surely that night in the Garden of Gethsemane when He agonized over His impending death, the same night in which He was betrayed. In that time of great need, "there appeared an angel unto him from heaven, strengthening him" (Luke 22:43).

Look Carefully

What do angels do? They worship God. They direct men. They protect believers. Angels give information. Angels may be involved in carrying home the righteous when they die. Angels bring God's judgment on both the pagan and God's people. Angels may sometimes exercise a ministry of healing. God has used angels to provide the physical needs of His people. Angels do battle for God and His children. They strengthen and encourage His own.

Perhaps you think to yourself, *I wish I could see such great things for myself—to experience some of the things pointed out in the Bible.*

Yes, of course. But perhaps God has something different in store for you. He may want you on the giving end rather than on the receiving end. If an angel were to come to your door dressed in spectacular garments and radiating the glory of God, you would certainly invite him in and give gracious, loving service.

Suppose, however, that someone of low estate came to your home. How would you respond? Perhaps it would not be in the same way as if he were an angel. But remember Hebrews 13:2: "Be not forgetful to entertain strangers: for thereby some have entertained angels unawares."

So let's put this down as a final thing angels do: They may give you an unexpected opportunity to reach out with the love of God and become involved, personally, with one of this magnificent order of the Creator's handiwork.

4
WHAT ANGELS KNOW

What a person does is based on what he knows. From time to time, for example, scientists warn of an epidemic that is expected to strike the country. The government makes the announcement in the electronic and print media and holds out encouragement with the development of a new vaccine. So millions of people go to their doctors or to clinics to protect themselves against what may cause them much sickness and pain.

Suppose you are in a hotel and someone shouts, "Fire!" You run for the nearest emergency exit, acting on what you know.

What is true of men is also true of angels. In the last chapter, we surveyed some things angels do. Why do they act? Presumably they act on the basis of what they know.

My mind immediately recalls 2 Samuel 14:20. A woman said to King Saul, "My lord is wise, according to the wisdom of an angel of God, to know all things that are in the earth." I'm not at all sure Saul was a wise man, based on some of the foolish things he did, but I am sure of the correctness of the woman's assessment of angels. Angels do indeed possess superhuman knowledge.

Where do angels get their knowledge? Directly from God Himself. He is the source of their intelligence. Their information comes directly from the throne of God, and that's the best of all wisdom in the universe.

Angels Know God Personally

Perhaps the chief thing angels know is God Himself. They know Him personally. They have a vital, intimate relationship with the Creator of all things. We have already seen time and again in this book that angels dwell in God's presence, surrounding His throne, worshiping Him.

When we consider further that true knowledge of God requires obedience to His commandments (see 1 John 2:3-5), we can better appreciate the ability of the holy angels to know God. Because they obey His commandments, they can more fully know Him. The mind of man was darkened by the Fall in the Garden of Eden, but those angels who remained loyal to God in the rebellion of Lucifer have had no such shades drawn over their understanding.

Angels Know the Reality of Demons

In addition to knowing God, angels also know
the reality of demons. They know how Lucifer
fell from heaven. They observed the many angels who elected to go with him and rebel
against God, a subject we shall consider in more
depth in Chapter 8. They know that spiritual
warfare is still going on between the forces of God
and the forces of Satan, a war that will continue
until Satan and his followers are cast into hell for
all eternity.

Now, what can we learn from this? I think angels are smarter than we are in regard to how to
wage spiritual warfare. They know there is a
war on, they are aware of it every day, and they
are able to discern the devil's traps. A good
place for us to start in our preparation for that
struggle is Ephesians 6:10-18.

Angels Know Human Beings

Not only do angels know God and their demonic adversaries, but they also know mankind, they know human beings. The Bible tells
us they were present at the creation of our physical universe (see Job 38:6,7), which logically
implies that they had already been created at
that point. So their knowledge of humanity began, I'm sure, with the very first pair to live on
earth. I'm certain the angels observed Adam

and Eve as they lived together in the Garden of Eden, tended the garden, and eventually sinned and had to be driven out of the garden. And we can be sure that those immortal creatures have been watching mankind ever since, often interacting with men and women at God's command.

Angels Knew of the Resurrection

As we study the biblical records, we observe that angels had to know of the resurrection. Certainly those angels who watched over the Lord during His earthly stay heard His repeated statements that He was going to be crucified and resurrected on the third day (see Matt. 12:40; 16:21; 17:9,22,23; 20:18,19).

Not only did an angel announce the Lord's resurrection to the women who first came to the tomb (see Matt. 28:5,6), but he had already rolled the stone away from the door of the tomb (see Matt. 28:2,3). Even prior to that, you remember that back when the angel appeared to Joseph to tell him to go ahead and marry Mary even though she was pregnant, the reason the angel gave was that "that which is conceived in her is of the Holy Ghost. And she shall bring forth a son, and thou shalt call his name JESUS: for he shall save his people from their sins" (Matt. 1:20,21). The angel knew the Lord was coming to save us from our sins, and we can infer that the angel knew our Lord had to die and be resurrected in order to purchase our salvation (see 1 Cor. 15).

When the Lord ascended into heaven some fifty days after the Resurrection, angels knew all about it. In fact, they had to nudge the apostles to tell them that, for the moment, their face-to-face encounter with Jesus was over. "And while they [the apostles] looked steadfastly toward heaven as he went up, behold, two men stood by them in white apparel; which also said, Ye men of Galilee, why stand ye gazing up into heaven? this same Jesus, which is taken up from you into heaven, shall so come in like manner as ye have seen him go into heaven" (Acts 1:10,11).

Angels Know the Purpose of God

The ultimate plan of God is to save men and women from their sins. To do that, He provided salvation through the Lord Jesus Christ, His Son. If you were asked to explain salvation to someone who had never heard of it, you probably could, given sufficient time.

Yet there are some things about salvation that are unexplainable because they are of such magnitude. Peter spoke of that fact in his first letter:

Of which salvation the prophets have inquired and searched diligently, who prophesied of the grace that should come unto you: searching what, or what manner of time the Spirit of Christ which was in them did signify, when it testified beforehand the sufferings of Christ, and the glory that should follow. Unto whom it was revealed, that not unto themselves, but unto us they did minister the things, which are now reported unto you by them that have preached the gospel unto you with the Holy Ghost sent down from heaven; which things the angels desire to look into (1 Pet. 1:10-12).

Angels, of course, transcend the times of the prophets. They have watched the unfolding of God's plan of salvation over the centuries, the millenia. They know it is the greatest possible theme of men or of angels. And although they know of salvation from an objective viewpoint (but not an experiential viewpoint, since angels don't need to be saved), they long to know it even more thoroughly.

Angels Know the Ministry of the Church

If we are not active participants in the churches we attend, we may not be aware of everything the church is or should be doing in its service to Christ. The angels of God, however, are well aware of the work and witness God ordained for the church. How do we know this? We know it from such passages as one in Paul's first letter to Timothy. Paul there set forth the things that Timothy was to do as a minister of the gospel. Paul summed up that section with these words: "I charge thee before God, and the Lord Jesus Christ, and the elect angels, that thou observe these things without preferring one before another, doing nothing by partiality" (1 Tim. 5:21). That's a fascinating and even a somber thought—to recognize that angels view what is going on in the local church and how it follows or fails to follow the directives God has given it.

Angels Know the Certainty of Judgment

We live in an increasingly secular society. Lawmakers, jurists, and humanists have done a great deal over the past half-century to banish God from public acknowledgment and recognition. And we have by no means seen the end of this tragic movement.

If there is no God, there is no need to live responsibly as if there were one. Man is free to do his own thing, to live it up, to enjoy all the pleasures his body can stand or his pocketbook can afford. And so we are seeing a complete abandonment of moral values.

If man thinks of death at all, he conceives of it as a cessation of being, perhaps a final period. But there is no way we can get around the finality of Hebrews 9:27, which reads, "It is appointed unto men once to die, but after this the judgment."

Unsaved people and even liberal churchmen deny the truth that is taught there. It's unpopular, unsettling, but angels are persuaded of the fact and know, as we have seen in Revelation, that they will take part in God's judgment. Indeed, they know that the final destination of unrepentant men and women, hell, is a place prepared originally for their number who disobeyed God and joined Satan's rebellion. Jesus foretold to His disciples what He would one day say at the time of judgment: "Then shall he say also unto them on the left hand, Depart from me, ye cursed, into everlasting fire, prepared for the devil and his angels" (Matt. 25:41).

What must angels think as they look down on earth and observe people laughing and taking their pleasure while, unknowingly, they rush headlong down the path to eternal destruction?

5
ANGELS
AND PROPHECY

One of the greatest human needs is that of self-revelation. John Donne's famous statement "No man is an island" is certainly true. We have a need to reveal ourselves to others. We need others to reveal themselves to us. Man is a social being and cannot find true happiness or fulfillment in himself alone.

God made us that way. In fact, God Himself seems to have a similar need, if we may speak of God as having needs. God is the original self-revelator. The term sounds strange, but it depicts accurately the fact that God has always been disclosing Himself. He did that, for example, in creating the natural world that, although marred by sin, contains such beauty. No wonder the psalmist exclaimed, "The heavens declare the glory of God; and the firmament showeth his handiwork" (Ps. 19:1).

God reveals Himself and His plans in many ways. In the past, He has talked directly with the leaders of His people and the prophets sent to them. Visions and dreams are other means

God has used to communicate with men. We have already looked at a number of cases in which angels delivered prophetic messages to men and women. In this chapter, we want to look at a few more specific cases of that important angelic activity.

A Coming Destruction

The ultimate self-revelation, of course, came about in the person of God's Son, for as the writer of Hebrews stated it, God "hath in these last days spoken unto us by his Son, whom he hath appointed heir of all things, by whom also he made the worlds" (Heb. 1:2).

God's Son was active in history, however, long before He came to this earth as a babe in Bethlehem. Sometimes He came down from heaven in a pre-incarnate visit (called a "theophany" or, more specifically, a "Christophany"). We do not know if it was in the same body in which He would later appear as a man for His thirty-three years on earth, but perhaps that was the case.

Sometimes He came in the company of angels. That was true when one day He appeared while Abraham was seated in his tent door. "And he [Abraham] lift up his eyes and looked, and, lo, three men stood by him" (Gen. 18:2). One was the Lord Jesus, I believe, and the other two were angels.

Why had they come? For two reasons: The first was to reassure Sarah that she would become the mother of the long-promised son of Abraham.

We infer the second reason from Genesis 18:17,18: "And the LORD said, Shall I hide from Abraham that thing which I do; seeing that Abraham shall surely become a great and mighty nation, and all the nations of the earth shall be blessed in him?" Here was the Lord talking with angels about whether Abraham should be brought in on the coming destruction of Sodom. So it seems evident that those angels participated in this prophetic revelation to Abraham, giving him advance information that the wicked city in which Lot, his nephew, lived would be destroyed. That gave opportunity to Abraham to intercede for Sodom, but in vain. The angels left the Lord and Abraham on a hilltop, left them to go and rescue Lot and his family before God destroyed the city.

Angels Ascending and Descending

God also spoke directly to Abraham's grandson, Jacob. Jacob, as you recall, was fleeing from home because he feared the wrath of his brother, Esau, for stealing the blessing of their father. Finally exhausted, Jacob lay down to sleep, cradling his head on a rock. "And he dreamed, and behold a ladder set up on the earth, and the top of it reached to heaven: and behold the angels of God ascending and descending on it" (Gen. 28:12).

It is hard to picture that dream in our own minds as God gave Jacob a special prophecy regarding the course of his life and what would happen to his descendants. Perhaps the angels stood by in solemn witness as God reminded Jacob of the Abrahamic covenant:

I am the LORD God of Abraham thy father, and the God of Isaac: the land where on thou liest, to thee will I give it, and to thy seed. . . . And, behold, I am with thee, and will keep thee in all places whither thou goest, and will bring thee again into this land; for I will not leave thee, until I have done that which I have spoken to thee of (Gen. 28:13,15).

In the many decades that he lived following that revelation, Jacob saw the fulfillment of the word God had spoken and to which the angels had been witness. And no doubt he reported the vision of God and the heavenly messengers to the sons God later gave him.

A Coming Mighty Man

After the death of Joshua, there was a time in the history of Israel when God used judges to guide His people. From time to time, angels, or, specifically, the angel of the Lord (perhaps a reference to the pre-incarnate Christ), were involved. The story of Manoah and his wife is a good example. One day this godly woman was visited by the angel, who said,

> Behold now, thou art barren, and bearest not: but thou shalt conceive, and bear a son. . . . and no razor shall come on his head: for the child shall be a Nazarite unto God from the womb: and he shall begin to deliver Israel out of the hand of the Philistines (Judg. 13:3,5).

To whom was the angel of the Lord referring? It was none other than Samson, who became one of the most noted judges of Israel and whose name even in secular society denotes superhuman strength. Here we see the Lord encouraging His people by giving them hope that one would come to free them from their bondage.

Angel at His Side

Zechariah, who wrote the book called by his name, is known as one of the minor prophets — minor in that the prophecies he gave are confined to a few short chapters compared to the books of Jeremiah or Isaiah.

How did Zechariah get his knowledge of what would come to pass? Some twenty times in the thirteen short chapters Zechariah wrote, the word *angel* appears. Often the heavenly messenger is described in the phrase, "the angel that talked with me." What a picturesque description—this man of God, asking questions about God's program, and receiving answers from "the angel that talked with me"!

Still Speaking Today?

It is easy to relegate all angelic activity with regard to prophecy to the ancient past. "But what of today?" you might ask. "Are angels still giving us revelations from God? Do they work with us in our service to the Lord Jesus?"

I believe they do. Although I can't prove that, let me give you a personal illustration that will help to explain my belief. Some years ago, I was flying from the Holy Land to New York City aboard a giant Boeing 747. I was using the time to study my Bible and prepare studies such as these.

A lady approached me, tapped me on the shoulder, and introduced herself. She was a widow of perhaps sixty years of age. "I was praying," she said, "and the Lord told me to tell you something."

"Yes?" I replied.

"The Lord told me that He would send His angels and would clear and release the American airways from demon power and possession in order that Christian television could go through and allow you to preach the gospel of Christ to millions of people in these last days."

I thanked her and returned to my studies.

About thirty minutes later, she came back. "I was praying again," she said, "and the Lord said you didn't listen to me the first time."

Inwardly, I had to admit that had been the case. I had not listened with my full attention, either of head or of heart.

"Now listen to me," she continued. "The Lord wants me to impress upon you that angels are going to release and to clear the American airways from demon power and possession." She reiterated her previous communication about how it would be my privilege to use television to reach the lost with the message of salvation.

This time, her words got through to me. "I thank you. I thank you very much," I replied, "and I, too, will pray."

I bowed my head and began to talk to the Lord about that very wonderful thing that had been communicated to me through prophecy. My soul rejoiced because I believed that that very thing would come to pass.

Just a few days later, I received word from the government that the license I had been seeking had been granted. The Lord brought to my mind the words I had heard: "I have freed the airways so that you can use them." I have no doubt that angels are assisting in this work.

I find that tremendously exciting. Angels

had something to do with that prophecy that came to me. And God allows the angels to clear the path of obstacles that may prevent us from doing the work of our heavenly Father.

Don't think that it could not be *your* privilege to work with angels in these last days.

Even if you should not have some personal experience with angels and prophecy, however, you need to know how God will use angels in the future, as given to us in the Book of Revelation. I will talk about that in some detail in the next chapter.

6
ANGELS IN
THE LIFE OF JESUS

When we consider those events in human history that have changed the world, there are really very few. Chief among those that do rank in that category, however, is the coming and walking among us of God Himself in the person of Jesus Christ. Certainly those were the most remarkable thirty-three years of all time.

Given the extraordinary nature of the Incarnation and the importance of the mission Christ came to accomplish, it is not surprising that angels were very much in evidence in association with the birth, life, death, and resurrection of the Lord. If ever there was a life in which angels had cause to be involved, it was the life of the Lord Jesus.

In this chapter, we want to look specifically at how angels were involved in the earthly life of Christ. We have already mentioned most of the relevant Scripture passages in earlier chapters, but we want to bring them together here with a few others and focus in one place on the role of angels in the life of the most remarkable man in history, God in human form.

Telling of His Prophet

The story of angelic involvement in the life of Christ really has to start before we even look at Mary and Joseph, for God had ordained that a prophet should go before the Messiah, both to announce His coming and to prepare the hearts and minds of the people for Him. And in His wisdom and sovereignty, God decided that the birth of this prophet should itself be a miracle.

The parents chosen for the prophet were Zacharias, a priest, and his wife, Elisabeth. They had never had children because Elisabeth was barren, and now they were also beyond the child-bearing years (see Luke 1:7. Notice also how closely this account parallels the case of Abraham and Sarah in Gen. 18:11,12). But God sent the angel Gabriel to Zacharias, as we saw earlier, to announce that not only would he and Elisabeth have a child, but also that their child would be the Messiah's forerunner, John the Baptist.

Later, when John the Baptist and Jesus were grown, John did indeed prepare the people for Christ, pointing out their sins and calling for repentance. And when Christ was ready to begin His public ministry and John's work was through, John said, "Ye yourselves bear me witness, that I said, I am not the Christ, but that I am sent before him. . . . He must increase, but I must decrease" (John 3:28,30).

Telling of His Coming

Angelic involvement in Christ's life continued before He was born, for His birth was to be a unique act, a new life conceived apart from the normal human process, without a man, in a virgin. Certainly the woman who was to bear the Christ-child had to be told before the fact; she had to be prepared for an event that was impossible apart from the intervention of God. Also, even though the event was to be an act of the Holy Spirit, it might expose the young woman to the taunts and abuse of those among her family and neighbors who did not believe in the miraculous nature of the conception. Indeed, fornication, which would be the only normal way for an unmarried woman to become pregnant, was punishable by death under Mosaic Law (see Lev. 20:10).

Therefore, God sent the angel Gabriel again, this time to tell the virgin Mary what was about to happen (see Luke 1:26-38). When Gabriel gave her the news, Mary was understandably perplexed. Gabriel explained, however, that it was the power of God Himself who would cause it to happen.

Notice Mary's reaction, then, to the news: "Behold the handmaid of the Lord; be it unto me according to thy word" (Luke 1:38). Next read Mary's beautiful Magnificat to see how thrilled she was to play such a part in God's eternal plan (see Luke 1:46-55). What a lesson she gives us of obedience and willingness to be used by God in whatever way He sees fit!

After Mary was found to be pregnant with the Christ-child, Joseph, her betrothed husband, wanted to put her away secretly to protect her from shame. Surely Mary had told him how the pregnancy had come about, but apparently he was having trouble believing it. So an angel was sent to reassure Joseph of the miraculous, godly nature of Mary's pregnancy and to encourage him to take her as his wife. Joseph obeyed, giving us another example of gracious obedience to God (see Matt. 1:18-23).

Announcing His Birth

The next part in the story of angels in the life of Jesus is very familiar to all of us. When the Christ-child was born in Bethlehem, God sent an angel to shepherds in a nearby field to announce His birth, "good tidings of great joy" of the coming of a Savior (see Luke 2:10-12).

As if that had not been enough to generate fear and awe in the hearts of the shepherds, after the angel told them where to locate the child, a multitude of angels appeared with the first angel, praising God and saying, "Glory to God in the highest, and on earth peace, good will toward men" (Luke 2:13,14).

Try to imagine yourself in that situation. Think what it must have looked and felt like. Then perhaps you can regain some of the wonder of that first Christmas. Think, too, of the overflowing joy and amazement the angels must have felt as they proclaimed that their Creator-God now lived among men as a tiny baby.

Protecting Him as a Baby

Jesus was born during the reign of King Herod, one of the family of Herods who ruled Palestine for several generations under Roman authority. When the three wise men came from the east to Jerusalem in search of the new King of the Jews, Herod called in the Jewish priests and scribes to ask where the Messiah was to be born. He then asked the three wise men when the star had appeared that had led them there (see Matt. 2:4-7).

Herod's motivations in asking those things, of course, were fear of a potential rival for the throne and a desire to eliminate that rival immediately. God knew that and understood that the life of the baby Jesus was in danger. So we read in Matthew 2:13 that when the wise men had left, "the angel of the Lord appeareth to Joseph in a dream, saying, Arise, and take the young child and his mother, and flee into Egypt, and be thou there until I bring thee word: for Herod will seek the young child to destroy him."

Joseph was again obedient to angelic instruction and took Mary and Jesus to Egypt (see Matt. 2:14). Then, as God had known would happen, Herod ordered the execution of every boy two years old and under in Bethlehem and the surrounding area (see Matt. 2:16). Herod figured that if he killed all the young boys, he would be sure to get the one whom he feared might overthrow him as king.

After Herod died and it was safe for Jesus and His family to return to Israel, "an angel appeareth in a dream to Joseph in Egypt, saying, Arise, and take the young child and his mother, and go into the land of Israel: for they are dead which sought the young child's life" (Matt. 2:19,20). So we see that once again, angels were watching over this special child and protecting Him from those who would harm Him.

Sustaining Him in His Ministry

We are told very little in the Bible of the years when Jesus was growing into an adult. No mention is made of any angelic activity in His life after those events surrounding His birth, although it would not be at all surprising if we were to learn in heaven that they ministered to Him many times in those years.

We next see angels ministering to Him, however, in the familiar story of His temptation in the wilderness, when He was beginning His public ministry. He had been led into the wilderness by the Holy Spirit, and there He fasted forty days and forty nights (see Matt. 4:1,2). While He was there, Satan came and tempted Him, failing every time. When Satan finally gave up and left, "angels came and ministered unto him [Jesus]" (Matt. 4:11).

Later, when Christ was in terrible agony of soul in the Garden of Gethsemane, struggling with the fact of His impending death for the sins of humanity, "there appeared an angel unto him from heaven, strengthening him" (Luke 22:43). If ever someone needed such help, it was the holy Son of God at that moment as He faced the prospect of bearing the sins of the world and dying on a cross. And an angel was there to provide that help.

Later, when Jesus was being arrested, He gave us insight into the angelic forces that were at His disposal should He need them. When the soldiers came to take Jesus, Peter had drawn a sword and cut off the ear of one of the high priest's servants who was with the soldiers (see Matt. 26:51; also John 18:10). Jesus, wanting to make clear to Peter that He was going to His death voluntarily, told him, "Thinkest thou that I cannot now pray to my Father, and he shall presently give me more than twelve legions of angels?" (Matt. 26:53). In other words, He was telling Peter, "It is not as though I am defenseless. All the angels I could possibly need to rescue Me are ready and waiting to do so if I so choose. I am being arrested of My own free will."

That statement from Jesus impresses upon us the fact that Christ truly did bear our sins willingly, demonstrating His love for us "while we were yet sinners" (Rom. 5:8). He had a choice; the angels were standing by to save Him; but He elected to die in our place.

Active in the Resurrection

The life and ministry of the Lord Jesus Christ did not end when He was crucified, for after death came the resurrection. The role of angels in His life continued as well.

When Jesus arose from the grave, "there was a great earthquake: for the angel of the Lord descended from heaven, and came and rolled back the stone from the door, and sat upon it. His countenance was like lightning, and his raiment white as snow. And for fear of him the keepers did shake, and became as dead men" (Matt. 28:2-4).

Picture yourself as one of those guards, and

perhaps then you can appreciate a little better how they must have felt when that angel appeared and rolled the stone away from the mouth of the tomb.

After that, the angelic role continued, for angels next had the privilege of announcing Christ's resurrection to His disciples. All the synoptic Gospels give us accounts of how the angels told the women who came to the tomb that Jesus was no longer there, that He had risen as He had said He would and as the Old Testament prophets had foretold (see Matt. 28:5-7; Mark 16:5-7; Luke 24:3-7). The gospel writers did not state it explicitly, but I am sure those angels must have been overflowing with joy as they gave the women that amazing, wonderful news.

Proclaiming and Participating in His Return

After forty days in His resurrected body, Jesus ascended into heaven, and again angels were involved. As Jesus' disciples watched Him ascend, two angels appeared beside them (see Acts 1:9,10). The angels prophesied, "This same Jesus, which is taken up from you into heaven, shall so come in like manner as ye have seen him go into heaven" (Acts 1:11).

What the angels did not say on that occasion, but which both Jesus and the apostle Paul affirmed, was that when Christ does indeed return to earth, the angels will come with Him. For example, Jesus said in Matthew 25:31, "When the Son of man shall come in his glory, and all the holy angels with him, then shall he sit upon the throne of his glory" (see also Mark 8:38; 2 Thess. 1:7). So we see that even in Jesus' future glorification upon the earth, angels will be involved, just as they were with Him and ministered to Him during His Incarnation.

7
ANGELS IN
THE REVELATION

If you discover one word used seventy-two times in one book of the Bible, you can safely assume that God considers it very important. Open a concordance to the entries for "angel" and "angels," begin to count, and you may be amazed to discover that the last portion of the New Testament, the Revelation, has far more to say about angelic activity than any other portion of God's Word.

In one sense, angels are "bookends" for the Revelation, and you understand that I say that reverently. Look at chapter 1, verse 1: "The Revelation of Jesus Christ, which God gave unto him, to show unto his servants things which must shortly come to pass; and he sent and signified it by his angel unto his servant John."

When we turn to the final chapter, in the last section of verses, angels appear again, holding the Revelation in a single, tight unit. They are pointed out by our Lord Himself: "I Jesus have sent mine angel to testify unto you these things in the churches" (Rev. 22:16).

The Book of Revelation is generally a chronological unfolding of future events, so let us look at angels in Revelation as their ministry progressively unfolds.

More than ten percent of the references to angels are found in connection with the letters to the seven churches in chapters 2 and 3. It's fascinating to consider that God might have detailed angels to carry messages to specific congregations. The meaning of "angel" in those references to the seven churches is not entirely clear, since "angel" literally means "messenger" and the word here could conceivably mean something like "pastor." However, these references could also be to the spiritual beings we have been studying.

Up to the Throne

You will recall that on one occasion the apostle Paul was caught up into the third heaven. He testified that he "heard unspeakable words, which it is not lawful for a man to utter" (2 Cor. 12:4).

We must be very careful in any speculation about what Paul referred to there. But it's just possible that he was allowed to witness, in a prophetic vision, what is described in Revelation

7:11,12 concerning angels. "And all the angels stood round about the throne,...saying, Amen: Blessing, and glory, and wisdom, and thanksgiving, and honor, and power, and might, be unto our God for ever and ever. Amen."

Did Paul see and hear the angels? I don't know, of course, but if he did, I think he would say it was simply indescribable in glory and majesty.

We have looked previously at the fact that one of the chief functions of angels is to worship God. We see in Revelation that they will have that privilege throughout eternity.

Executing Judgment

How disappointing it is to end our view of that heavenly scene and let our eyes again focus on things of earth. Here, instead of angels praising God, we see men and women blaspheming God and living in sin, with no sense of obligation to God.

Why is that? At least a partial answer is found in Ecclesiastes 8:11: "Because sentence against an evil work is not executed speedily, therefore the heart of the sons of men is fully set in them to do evil."

In this age of grace, all men benefit from the longsuffering and patience of God. He does not immediately punish sin, but there is coming a day when He will, and He will use angels as agents of His vengeance. In an earlier chapter, we had already looked briefly at angels as instruments of God's judgment. Let's focus now on their activity in that role in the Book of Revelation.

Angelic Warnings, Angelic Reapings

The angelic job of warning people and then, if the warning is not heeded, bringing about the judgment of God will be especially in force during the end times in relationship to the antichrist.

Let me begin to explain the above by quoting from Revelation 14.

> And the third angel followed them, saying with a loud voice, If any man worship the beast and his image, and receive his mark in his forehead, or in his hand, the same shall drink of the wine of the wrath of God, which is poured out without mixture into the cup of his indignation; and he shall be tormented with fire and brimstone in the presence of the holy angels, and in the presence of the Lamb: and the smoke of their torment ascendeth up for ever and ever: and they have no rest day nor night, who worship the beast and his image, and whosoever receiveth the mark of his name (vv. 9-11).

During his brief reign on earth, Antichrist is going to control completely the economic life of everyone. No one will be able to buy or sell unless he has a mark on his forehead or his hand. So people will have to make a decision— whether to identify themselves with God's people and suffer death as the consequence, or whether to go along with Antichrist. The great majority will make the wrong choice. They will say, "I'm ready. Give me the mark."

Then, like a dam that is broken, the fury of God will spring forth. Notice how angels are involved:

> And another angel came out of the temple, crying with a loud voice to him that sat on the cloud, Thrust in thy sickle, and reap: for the time is come for thee to reap; for the harvest of the earth is ripe. And he that sat on the cloud thrust in his sickle on the earth; and the earth was reaped. And another angel came out of the temple which is in heaven, he also having a sharp sickle. And another angel came out from the altar, which had power over fire; and cried with a loud cry to him that had the sharp sickle, saying, Thrust in thy sharp sickle, and gather the clusters of the vine of the earth; for her grapes are fully ripe. And the angel thrust in his sickle into the earth, and gathered the vine of the earth, and cast it into the great winepress of the wrath of God. And the winepress was trodden without the city, and blood came out of the winepress, even unto the horse bridles, by the space of a thousand and six hundred furlongs (Rev. 14:15-20).

What a terrible picture that is of God's coming judgment, but one that is fully deserved. Now we think of angels as blessing the world and strengthening and guiding us down here. They do, but there is coming a time when angels will be dealing out the wrath of a righteous God. Where do you stand just now, under the present blessing of angels or under the coming judgment?

I pray that every reader of this book might come to know the Lord Jesus Christ as his or her personal savior. My words to you may not be effective, but will you receive warning from the Word of God? I urge you to get a Bible and read the sixteenth chapter of Revelation, which is too long for me to quote here. You will note how seven angels are used by God to execute His fierce wrath upon an unbelieving world. It's a terrible, terrible picture of things to come, and I would have you avoid it at all costs.

Babylon, Babylon

God is not only going to judge individuals during the Great Tribulation, but He is also going to bring judgment on world systems. Two Babylons are mentioned in Revelation, one in chapter 17 and one in chapter 18.

First to be judged is religious Babylon. We cannot be certain of its exact identity. But I want you to see how an angel was involved in giving John information. He wrote, "And there came one of the seven angels which had the seven vials, and talked with me, saying unto me, Come hither; I will show unto thee the judgment of the great whore that sitteth upon many waters" (Rev. 17:1). So an angel gave the apostle a preview of the judgment that is to come on that false religious system.

Even more striking is the angelic involvement with regard to the second, or economic, Babylon, described in Revelation 18.

> And after these things I saw another angel come down from heaven, having great power; and the earth was lightened with his glory. And he cried mightily with a strong voice, saying, Babylon the great is fallen, is fallen, and is become the habitation of devils, and the hold of every foul spirit, and a cage of every unclean and hateful bird (vv. 1,2).

That is a remarkable prophecy having to do with the tribulation period. Nowhere else is an angel described quite like that. His mission is to judge economic Babylon. Some say it is New York City or the United Nations; we can't know for sure. But our point here is to emphasize the angelic involvement.

An Angel in the Sun

Artists often picture angels as having a bright

countenance. Where do they get that idea? Perhaps from Revelation 19:17: "And I saw an angel standing in the sun." That seems to refer to a brilliance that shone from his face. What a sight that would be!

I don't think our eyes would remain on the angel for long, however, because this one, too, has a work of judgment to execute. The rest of Revelation 19 tells how the remains of a great army provide food for the fowls, and then how at last, the beast and the false prophet and those who worshiped his image are all cast into a lake of fire burning with brimstone.

The preceding have been just some highlights of angelic involvement in the judgments described in Revelation. You will want to read the entire Book of Revelation for yourself to appreciate all that angels will be doing in the end times. Pay special attention to those passages that have not been discussed much in this study as they relate to judgment—for example, chapters 4-13, 20-22.

8
WHAT KIND OF PEOPLE RECEIVE ANGELIC SERVICE?

Whenever you hear of something good coming your way, something desirable, you may ask yourself, "I wonder if I will receive it? I wonder if I am eligible?" Perhaps you have raised those questions in connection with our study on angels. So, we need to consider together who receives the services of angels.

As we begin this chapter, we need to keep in the front of our minds the sovereignty of God. He cannot be made to jump through a hoop, even if we think we have satisfied some list of requirements. He is God, not us; His understanding is perfect, not ours. And we know that with His perfect understanding of our lives and needs, He is causing all things to work together for our ultimate good (see Rom. 8:28).

What we will be looking at in this chapter, then, are some general characteristics of people or situations for whom or in which God has provided angelic intervention in the past. There is no foolproof formula for getting angelic assistance. Even pagans, people who are anti-God, sometimes receive angelic aid. (Remember the warning given to Babylonian King Nebuchadnezzar?)

Given those cautions, let's look at a few examples of who receives angelic service. We have looked at some of these people and situations before, but now we want to look behind the scenes at motivations and causes.

Those Who Know and Serve God

Angels help those who know and serve God. That makes the scope very large. Do you have a knowledge of God by virtue of being related to Him through His Son, Jesus Christ? If you do, you have been born again. You are on speaking terms with God, and the channels are open. God can now give you spiritual manifestations, such as the visitation of angels.

I began the first chapter of this book by relating a story from my boyhood years, and I briefly refer to it again here. I told how a stranger once came to our door and asked to be fed. My mother agreed, provided the meal, and then sensed something unusual about him. Right after he left she opened the door, but he was nowhere in sight. Mother became aware that she may have been entertaining an angel, after the manner described in Hebrews 13:2.

That would not surprise me at all. My mother knew God—really knew Him. She knew and loved His Word. She knew and loved His Son. She was one of the most devoted women to prayer and to the reading of the Bible that I have ever met.

Do you long for the things of God? Do you have a hunger to know Him better? Perhaps, for example, you hear the verse "I was glad when they said unto me, Let us go into the house of the LORD" (Ps. 122:1), and you reply, "Yes, let's go!" That's evidence that you are seeking God and all He has for you.

If you know God, you probably will serve Him as well. But suppose you were to learn, to your utter amazement and fear, that the government had just passed a law saying you could no longer pray to God? Would that change your prayer habits? You might excuse yourself by recalling that verse which speaks of going into a closet to pray. You might reason that if it were suddenly illegal to pray, it would be a good time for closet prayer. That is not true service to God, however.

Indeed, that very law was passed during the time of Daniel. The complete story is told in the sixth chapter of the book that bears his name. Did Daniel go to his walk-in closet and there pour out his petitions to God? "Now when Daniel knew that the writing was signed, he went into his house; and his windows being open in his chamber toward Jerusalem, he kneeled upon his knees three times a day, and prayed, and gave thanks before his God, as he did aforetime" (v. 10).

It is true that for breaking the king's law, Daniel was thrown into the den of lions. But he met an angel there and felt right at home, as we observed earlier. You see, Daniel served God devoutly all his life.

As you would expect, we find many similar examples in Scripture — accounts of God's servants who received angelic visitations. Mary, the human mother of our Lord, was such a person. She loved God; she truly loved Him. (Read of her love and reverence for God in the Magnificat in Luke 1:47-55.) God selected her among all the women of the world for all time to be the mother of the baby Jesus. That willingness on her part would bring her malicious talk, embarrassment — even the possible loss of her betrothed — but Mary was devout, and Mary saw an angel.

Ezekiel was another example of those who served God. Some people pass up reading his book because they don't feel it has anything to say to them. In reading it, however, we weep with the prophet over the sins of God's people, and at the same time we find our hearts warmed as they get in tune with his great love for God. And Ezekiel saw angels.

Do you remember the story of Cornelius? He was a Roman centurion stationed in Israel.

What kind of man was he? The Bible says he was "a devout man, and one that feared God with all his house, which gave much alms to the people, and prayed to God always" (Acts 10:2). Cornelius meant business with God. He wasn't just playing around, biding his time until he could get back to Rome and enjoy the good life. He knew that God was worthy of being sought with all his heart, and Cornelius saw an angel.

Those Who Need God's Special Help

People who have special needs have often received angelic service very beautifully, wonderfully, and dynamically. Think of Joshua. He found himself at the head of the Israelite army. Although he had some military command experience under Moses, he had never before borne alone the entire load of leadership responsibility. He knew he needed help and that God was his only resource.

Does it surprise you that God came to Joshua's aid? Would you expect God to call down from heaven, "Sorry, but you're on your own"? No, of course not. Our heavenly Father wants to meet us at the point of our need, whatever that may be. Here, in Joshua's case, it was for military planning, and that's exactly what Joshua got.

How was that assistance and guidance given? Through the presence of an angel (see Josh. 5:13,14). No wonder Joshua was able to lead the people in a great victory!

Peter and the other apostles offer us another example. They found themselves in prison because they loved God and had been serving Him openly by preaching the Word faithfully. The Jewish religious leaders didn't like that. They had them cast into prison, but they were in for a shock. Why? Because

> the angel of the Lord by night opened the prison doors, and brought them forth.... But when the officers came, and found them not in the prison, they returned, and told, saying, The prison truly found we shut with all safety, and the keepers standing without before the doors: but when we had opened, we found no man within (Acts 5:19,22,23).

Some people might say, "Well, that was a long time ago. I don't think God works like that today to deliver His saints."

Oh, but He does, my friend! The outstanding Indian evangelist Sadhu Sundar Singh was in jail in Tibet for preaching the gospel in that far-off country. The Lama had placed him in confinement, and to make sure he wouldn't go out, the Lama personally kept the key on his belt, but an angel came, and he didn't need the key. The next day, the Lama looked for his prisoner, but he was nowhere to be found. You see, Sundar Singh needed to get out, and God sent an angel to accomplish it.

Are you convinced that angels are aware of our needs and are fully commissioned by God, as He directs, to meet those needs? Many sick people have seen angels during their sickness and have regained health. At other times, people who have been preaching have seen angels at the pulpit. Angels come in times of great pressure, great need.

I want to leave you with the clear understanding that God has met and can meet special needs through angels. I also feel a need at this point, however, to remind you that God, with a higher purpose in mind, does not always work as we would expect. Peter, Sundar Singh, and others have been miraculously delivered from bondage, for example, but many other godly people have not. Read all the way through Hebrews 11 to see what I mean. Consider also the many Christians who are suffering for their faith, even as you read this, in parts of the world where there is no freedom of worship.

In all these situations, we need to have the attitude of the three Israelite young men who refused to worship Nebuchadnezzar's golden image and so faced the prospect of being thrown into the fiery furnace. They told Nebuchadnezzar that they knew God could deliver them and that they thought He would (see Dan. 3:17). Then they said, "But if not, be it known unto thee, O king, that we will not serve thy gods, nor worship the golden image which thou hast set up" (Dan. 3:18). You see, they were prepared for and ready to accept the possibility that God might choose not to deliver them; and even if that happened, they were not going to worship Nebuchadnezzar's idol.

Perhaps you have thought to yourself, *I know God. I serve Him with all my heart. From time to time, I have special needs.* If so, it seems evident that you, too, fit in with the people who received angelic help during the biblical era.

Just how or when or even if God may choose to send you angelic assistance, I cannot say. However, I know He can. I know He has in the past, and that's just one of many things that make the Christian life so exciting and adventurous.

9
THE REBEL ANGELS

An entire volume could be devoted to the subject of Satan and his demonic angels. (I have, in fact, addressed this topic in my book *Demons: The Answer Book.*) But on these pages I would like to give you a brief overview of some things you should know, because God wants us to be informed about our adversaries.

Is He Real?

Many people question the reality of Satan. Some believe Satan is just a name for some sort of evil force in the universe that has no personality or individuality. Others think of Satan as just a character in stories who goes about in a red suit, carrying a pitchfork.

What does the Word of God say? It sets forth Satan as a person throughout the Old Testament. We run into this evil personage in the Garden of Eden (Gen. 3:1-15). We see him afflicting Job (See Job 1:6-19; 2:1-7). We detect his work among the heathen nations as described in many of the writers of prophecy.

What do we find in the New Testament? There he is again, in nineteen of the twenty-seven books that make up this portion of the Bible, and his existence is implied in the other books as well.

The Lord Jesus often spoke of the devil, and we could ask for no better authority.

As a person, you think, you feel, you act. Satan does the same. He gives every evidence of being a separate entity, as alive and as self-conscious as you are at this very moment.

Satan's Origin

It is only natural that you should ask where Satan came from. The Bible teaches us that "by him [Christ] were all things created, that are in heaven, and that are in earth, visible and invisible" (Col. 1:16). Satan is a created being.

Would our Lord make something evil, however, someone who has brought such curse and destruction on mankind? No. Satan developed into what he is today, but that's not the way he was in the beginning. Originally, Satan was an angel of great power and privilege. He was a perfect creature called "Lucifer, son of the morning" (Is. 14:12). He lived in the presence of God.

And read what Ezekiel wrote of Satan:

Thou sealest up the sum, full of wisdom, and perfect in beauty. Thou hast been in Eden the garden of God.... Thou art the anointed cherub that covereth; and I have set thee so: thou wast upon the holy mountain of God; thou hast walked up and down in the midst of the stones of fire. Thou wast perfect in thy ways from the day that thou wast created (Ezek. 28:12-15).

Satan's Fall

Then something happened. What was it? I broke off in the middle of the last verse quoted above. Let me finish it: " ... till iniquity was found in thee.... Thine heart was lifted up because of thy beauty" (vv. 15b, 17a). There is the answer. Satan was not content to remain as he was. He wanted to become "number one" — to replace God. This cherub who covered the throne of God, who protected the holiness of God, mounted a rebellion in paradise.

Can you picture in the eye of your mind that day in heaven so long ago when that event took place? The thought, the desire, the determination came to Satan, and he said in his heart, once pure but now turned to wickedness, "I will ascend into heaven, I will exalt my throne above the stars of God: I will sit also upon the mount of the congregation, in the sides of the north: I will ascend above the heights of the clouds; I will be like the most High" (Is.

14:13,14). What a decisive moment! What a
great catastrophe!

Angelic Choice

Let me digress for a moment and draw your
attention to a point that seems obvious and yet
deserves a brief mention.

We just saw that Satan, in his original creation, was perfect, as man had been in his original creation. But then, like man, Satan chose to
disobey God and go his own way.

The obvious and logical implication is that angels, like man, have a free will. They can choose
to obey or disobey God. They are not machines
programmed to respond in only one way. Those
who have remained in heaven in God's service
have chosen to obey Him; those who followed
Satan chose disobedience.

Out—Now, Forever

As we noted in an earlier chapter, Satan's
plan didn't work. God knew how to deal with his
rebellion. Those two verses quoted above are
preceded and followed by others that tell us
what happened: "How art thou fallen from heaven, O Lucifer, son of the morning! how art
thou cut down to the ground, which didst weak-
en the nations! ... Yet thou shalt be brought

down to hell, to the sides of the pit" (Is. 14:12,15).

Satan made five "I will" statements as recorded above in Isaiah, but God made six "I will" statements as found in Ezekiel:

> I will cast thee as profane out of the mountain of God: and I will destroy thee, O covering cherub, from the midst of the stones of fire. . . . I will cast thee to the ground, I will lay thee before kings, that they may behold thee. . . . therefore will I bring forth a fire from the midst of thee, it shall devour thee, and I will bring thee to ashes upon the earth in the sight of all them that behold thee (Ezek. 28:16-18).

God always has the last word. He makes the final statement.

Satan's Allies

From time to time, we read in the papers or see on television accounts of people who have risen up to overthrow their governments. Almost always, a wide conspiracy is involved. An individual can't do it by himself. He has to have help. He needs co-plotters, co-conspirators, co-revolutionaries.

Does it surprise you to learn, then, that when Satan was cast out of heaven, he didn't go alone? No, many of the angels joined Satan's cause. There is a suggestion of the number who did given in Revelation 12. We read there of a great red dragon, "and his tail drew the third part of the stars of heaven, and did cast them to the earth" (v. 4). So perhaps a third of all the angels God originally created decided to join Satan and were swept up in God's wrath and cast out of heaven.

It is those fallen angels who are now demons, or evil angels. Satan is their one and only leader. He is their commander in chief, their executive officer.

Satan's Work

Satan works in continual opposition to God's program and person, for he is the archenemy of God. He sets up counterfeit doctrine and religion. He doesn't mind, for example, that people go to church, so long as it is a church that doesn't preach, practice, or believe the gospel. Second Corinthians 4:3,4 teaches us that Satan blinds men to the truth that is in Christ.

As the great deceiver, Satan will misuse Scripture to try to get people to do wrong things while they think they're doing right, as he did when he tempted the Lord Jesus (see Matt. 4:1-11). He and his allies also disguise themselves as angels of light, or righteousness, in order to deceive and mislead people away from God (see 2 Cor. 11:13-15). Jesus described him as the father of lies (see John 8:44).

Have you ever considered ways in which Satan may affect you? For one thing, he is the "accuser of our brethren" (Rev. 12:10). He reminds God when we fall and sin. But how wonderful it is that we have an answering "advocate with the Father, Jesus Christ the righteous" (1 John 2:1).

Whenever trials and difficulties come into your life, you wonder about the goodness of God. Satan may be responsible for those thoughts. Remember? That's how he got to Eve (see Gen. 3:1-5).

Satan is the great tempter. He tempts us to lie, to engage in immorality, to kill.

Like Their Mentor

You have heard the expression "Like father, like son" I'm sure. You might say sometimes that a certain boy acts or speaks just like Harry. And sure enough, you find out that he is Harry's son.

Those in the devil's camp also have a family resemblance. Jesus spoke of those who acted like their father, the devil (see John 8:44), and that generalization applies especially to those angelic beings who were dismissed from heaven at the same time as Satan.

Like their boss, evil angels are also personalities who talk, think, feel, and act. The Bible calls them spirits (see Matt. 8:16) and calls us to battle against their wicked organization. "For we wrestle not against flesh and blood, but against principalities, against powers, against the rulers of the darkness of this world, against spiritual wickedness in high places" (Eph. 6:12).

Those morally perverted beings are often described in the Bible as "unclean spirits" (Matt. 10:1; Luke 11:24). I'm sure even that designation fails to convey all their wickedness and depravity.

A Long List

What do those rebel angels do? As the emissaries of Satan, their major job, from our perspective, is to oppose the saints of God. It is no wonder that that outstanding passage in Ephesians 6 sounds such a strident call for us to arm ourselves with the whole armor of God so that we may stand against the wiles of the devil. Verses 13-17 tell us of the armor available to us through the provision of God. We need to read that passage frequently and obey its injunctions.

Demons want us to return to the old life with all its sins. They tempt us to go back to the things from which we were set free at the time of our conversion. I'm sorry to say that in many cases, they apparently succeed. How many people do you know, formerly strong Christians, who have slid back from what they once were in Christ? Perhaps they are still in the church, but on a routine, formalistic basis.

Some people may even be drawn away altogether from the faith. "Now the Spirit speaketh expressly, that in the latter times some shall depart from the faith, giving heed to seducing spirits, and doctrines of devils; speaking lies in hypocrisy; having their conscience seared with a hot iron" (1 Tim. 4:1,2).

We often read in the Old Testament of how evil messengers from Satan turned the people of God to idolatry. We read, for example, of those who "offer their sacrifices unto devils, after whom they have gone a whoring" (Lev. 17:7).

Do you see the hands of evil angels at work in the false religions of the world? Think of the hundreds of millions of people—like the Muslims, for example—who hold with such zeal to their false doctrine and are marching unknowingly on the road to hell.

You don't have to go off to the Middle East or India to gain evidence of demons working on the double. In the United States alone, we have scores of cults that blind people to the truth and keep them out of the Kingdom of God. No doubt, much of this is due to the misleading of evil spirits. We need to underscore in our Bibles and in our thinking the words of John:

Beloved, believe not every spirit, but try the
spirits whether they are of God: because many
false prophets are gone out into the world.
Hereby know ye the Spirit of God: Every spirit
that confesseth that Jesus Christ is come in the
flesh is of God: And every spirit that confesseth not that Jesus Christ is come in the flesh is
not of God: and this is that spirit of antichrist,
whereof ye have heard that it should come; and
even now already is it in the world (1 John
4:1-3).

Afflicting the Body

Demons seem to have particular power to affect the human body. How often we see that
during the earthly ministry of our Lord. Here is
just one example from Matthew 12:22: "Then
was brought unto him one possessed with a devil, blind, and dumb: and he healed him, inso-
much that the blind and dumb both spake and
saw."

Do you remember the case of the epileptic
boy whose problem was caused by demonic
activity? Jesus gave him healing, as recorded in
Mark 9:17-27.

We have record in the Bible of a case of insan-
ity that was caused by devils. Dr. Luke recorded the incident of the man who roamed among
the tombs, naked and uncontrollable. At the
command of Jesus, the demons announced
their true identity, for there were many of

them, so many that they could be called Legion. It's a frightening story given in Luke 8:26-40.

Please understand that I am not saying that all physical or mental illness is the result of demonic activity—by no means. But some is, and we should recognize that.

Demonic Possession

Unfortunately, the demonic activity mentioned in the Bible continues into present times. Demons can enter and take possession of people. I can give you a couple of illustrations from my own experience. Some of the most exciting moments of my life and ministry have been when the power of God has released those possessed with evil spirits.

In the city where I presently serve, a woman from a liberal church came on a Sunday night and asked for prayer. When I laid my hands on her, I was startled to hear what sounded like the barking of a dog coming from her mouth. I also heard growling and other animal sounds.

God set her free from that demonic possession. Then I asked her how she had gotten into that terrible situation. She confessed that she had been dabbling in spiritism and playing with a Ouija board. She had given herself to the occult, and the evil spirits had taken over. It took a confrontation between God and the evil things to release her from bondage.

One time during my missionary years in the Philippines, I was asked to go to prison and pray for a young woman who gave every evidence of being demon-possessed. Skeptics knew I had been invited, so there were some 125 people on hand to observe what transpired—prison officials, newspaper reporters, university professors, and key people from the medical world.

When I arrived, I found the woman twisting and turning and screaming under the power of the devil. As I laid hands on her to pray, she began to blaspheme all three members of the Trinity. "Come out of her!" I commanded on the authority of God's Word.

You can imagine the impact it had on those who had come to watch. Newspapers and magazines carried the complete story. As a result of that one instance, that one deliverance of a person bound by Satan, a revival broke out in the land. Many came to know the Lord, and rich blessings followed.

All that stemmed from believing what our Lord Jesus said in Mark 16:17: "And these signs shall follow them that believe; In my name shall they cast out devils." The Book of Acts gives examples of this in biblical times, but I have seen the freeing of individuals in our time as well.

For You as Well

Every Christian has the power to exorcise evil spirits. Do you belong to Jesus Christ? He that is in you is greater than he that is in the world. You have the right to pray for those ensnared and see the demons cast out. When you believe that and trust God for it, you may see it happen if God so chooses to use you.

Do not be foolhardy as you confront Satan, however. God is indeed infinitely more powerful than him, but that does not mean Satan is weak. Much to the contrary, everything we said earlier about the power and intelligence of angels applies to Satan and his demons as well. Remember that before his rebellion, Lucifer was one of the most glorious and powerful of God's angels. Remember also that the Bible portrays him "as a roaring lion, walketh about, seeking whom he may devour" (1 Pet. 5:8). He is not an adversary to be lightly regarded by anyone.

Victory Assured

At this point, you may wonder what is to be the fate of those rebel angels. The Word of God is very clear on that issue. We have many statements that indicate God has already decided the matter through the victorious life and death of

The Rebel Angels

the Lord Jesus. For example, "For this purpose the Son of God was manifested, that he might destroy the works of the devil" (1 John 3:8). And now it is our part to wait for the sentence against the evil one and his angels to be carried out completely.

Part of the devil's band may already have been apprehended. Note the words of 2 Peter 2:4: "For if God spared not the angels that sinned, but cast them down to hell, and delivered them into chains of darkness, to be reserved unto judgment." Jude 6 has something similar to say: "And the angels which kept not their first estate, but left their own habitation, he hath reserved in everlasting chains under darkness unto the judgment of the great day." So a portion of the evil angels — how many we do not know — may already be under lock and key, prevented from ravaging the world and the saints.

What about those that are loose and still active? Their time is limited, and their doom is equally certain. But before that day comes, we are going to see Satan especially at work concerning the person of the Antichrist. "And then shall that Wicked be revealed, whom the Lord shall consume with the spirit of his mouth, and shall destroy with the brightness of his coming: Even him, whose coming is after the working of Satan with all power and signs and lying wonders" (2 Thess. 2:8,9).

The Final Defeat

The stage will then be set for the return of the Lord Jesus, and that event is marvelously described for us in Revelation 19.

> And I saw heaven opened, and behold a white horse; and he that sat upon him was called Faithful and True, and in righteousness he doth judge and make war. His eyes were as a flame of fire, and on his head were many crowns; and he had a name written, that no man knew, but he himself. And he was clothed with a vesture dipped in blood: and his name is called The Word of God. And the armies which were in heaven followed him upon white horses, clothed in fine linen, white and clean (Rev. 19:11-14).

What a magnificent picture of our sovereign Lord and His own!

John went on to give us a picture of Satan's fate: "And I saw an angel come down from heaven, having the key of the bottomless pit and a great chain in his hand. And he laid hold on the dragon, that old serpent, which is the Devil, and Satan, and bound him a thousand years" (Rev. 20:1,2).

At the end of that temporary sentence, Satan will be loosed for a little while to resume his old activity of deceiving the nations. But then the end will come: "And the devil that deceived them was cast into the lake of fire and brimstone, where the beast and the false prophet are, and shall be tormented day and night for ever and ever" (Rev. 20:10).

I find that comforting and reassuring. Today Satan and his evil forces wreak their destruction on individuals, on homes, on nations. But the day is coming when it shall all be over.

Our Lord is going to win. And we are going to win in Him. Meanwhile, let us be fully informed and draw closer to the One who gives us the victory.

10
YOUR PRIVATE ANGEL

Unless you are among the rich, you probably don't have enough money to buy services exclusively for yourself. But if you did, you might have a private chauffeur to drive you around town. You could have a private hair stylist to do everything possible to make you look your very best. You could hire a tutor to spend his time teaching you foreign languages or science. And in these days so filled with violent crime, you might want to get a personal bodyguard to protect your life.

I know something far better, however, that you can afford. In fact, you don't need money at all to enjoy fantastic personal services that God provides for you. The answer? Your private angel.

I cannot prove conclusively from Scripture the existence of private angels. There is no one passage of clear, unequivocal teaching on the subject. However, there are a few references that, taken together, seem to suggest strongly the reality of guardian angels. They are enough to convince me of the fact. Let's take a look at them. When we are finished, I think you will have an entirely new perspective that will make you eternally grateful to God.

For You Individually

I'm sure we often think of angels as being in general service to the entire body of Christ. Such a concept is not wrong. Angels do indeed minister to God's people as a whole. But they are also concerned for us as individuals.

When we look at Psalm 91:11, we begin to see the personal nature of angelic ministry: "For he shall give his angels charge over thee, to keep thee in all thy ways." Note that all those pronouns are singular. That is a first suggestion to me that each of us has a personal angel who watches over us. When we consider also that we who believe in Christ are indwelt by the Holy Spirit (see 1 Cor. 3:16), we can be sure that God is always very much aware of our needs and concerns and is able to minister to them.

Another suggestion of personal angels comes to us in Genesis 48:16, where a dying Jacob (Israel) was blessing his grandchildren, Joseph's sons. In that blessing, he referred to "the angel which redeemed me from all evil." Was that a guardian angel who had watched over Jacob throughout his lifetime? I like to think it was.

To the Rescue

Let me give you just one example of a time when God may have used my guardian angel to rescue me. Years ago, I was traveling with a group up near the border of Tibet. Somehow, I became lost—I mean absolutely lost. You know the feeling. I had been separated from my traveling companions from about 8:00 in the morning until about 4:30 that afternoon. There I was in a little Chinese village, all by myself, without knowing one word of the language. I was sad and tired, almost in tears.

Then I noticed a young man come riding through the gates of the village on a majestic horse. He rode right up to where I was, dismounted, and began to talk to me in perfect English.

"Where did you come from?" I asked. "How is it that you speak English so beautifully?"

He smiled and said to me, "I know the party you're looking for. I met them on the road. If you go out this gate and then go for about two hours, you'll find them ahead."

I took his advice. I got on my mule, headed out the gate, and, sure enough, before long I found the folks I had been traveling with.

I inquired of them about the young man. They told me they had never seen him. They didn't know anything about him.

Could that have been my guardian angel? I believe it was.

Very Close

You might wonder just how far away your personal angel is when you need him. We have an answer in Psalm 34:7, which tells us, "The angel of the LORD encampeth round about them that fear him, and delivereth them." That means your angel puts up his tent around you. If you fear God, you have an angel by your side to give protection. You don't have to be afraid of leaving him behind when you board a jet to travel across the country, or when you jump into your car for a quick trip to the supermarket. No, he is always there, and that should be comforting.

Children, Too

We may ignore little children or think they are not very important. But God has a different perspective. It was our Lord Himself who said, "Take heed that ye despise not one of these little ones; for I say unto you, That in heaven their angels do always behold the face of my Father which is in heaven" (Matt. 18:10). That is perhaps the strongest biblical suggestion that each child (and, by inference, each person) has a guardian angel all his own.

Perhaps little children are in greater need of

angelic protection than adults because they can't defend themselves as well. Do children need such protection? Just look through any metropolitan newspaper and you will get the sad answer. Child abuse is one of the greatest areas of social concern in this nation. It includes physical abuse, mental abuse, and even sexual abuse. Millions of children are the victims. It's something they can't easily shake off or forget. Whole lives may be ruined because of what happens in childhood.

God doesn't overlook what happens to children. His angels don't overlook it, and the day of accounting will most certainly come. I wonder if those who abuse or mislead children are aware of or believe God's promised judgment in Matthew 18:6: "But whoso shall offend one of these little ones which believe in me, it were better for him that a millstone were hanged about his neck, and that he were drowned in the depth of the sea."

More Than Enough

The concept of having a private angel might make you wonder whether there are enough angels to go around. It's perfectly proper to raise the question. Let me refer you to the Book of Daniel and his vision of the Ancient of days seated upon His throne, surrounded by angels:

"Thousand thousands ministered unto him, and ten thousand times ten thousand stood before him" (Dan. 7:10). That second figure, taken literally, is 100 million. We don't know if Daniel was being literal there; perhaps he was speaking symbolically of a huge, uncountable number. Regardless, the point here is that there are undoubtedly vast legions of angels at God's command.

You might say, "There are more than four billion people on the earth, and the number is growing. Are there enough angels to help them *all?*" I can only say that if we are right in concluding that God does assign a personal guardian angel to every individual, there must be enough angels to do the job. Certainly there is no doubt but that God was and is perfectly capable of creating all the angels He would ever want.

An Unequaled Record

I hope you feel on the victory side when you stop to consider that you have a personal angel. What an unparalleled record they have in their ministry to us. Angels never get too old to serve, too tired of the job, or too discouraged or sad to quit.

Never forget for even one moment your private angel or the intimate relationship with angels established by God to bless and help you. They come as friends and allies in the battle against Satan in your life.

11
ANGELS FOREVER

When I began to study angels prior to writing this book, I was guided by a theory that I refer to from time to time. I express it this way: God cannot bless ignorance. No, God wants us to be informed—to know what His Word says in every field of learning.

That theory needs to be applied in the study of angels. By and large, people are woefully ignorant. If you introduce the subject of angels, they may smile a little, recalling some incident involving angels in Old Testament times or perhaps in connection with the birth and later resurrection of our Lord. But they have no clear understanding of the role of angels in the past, in the present, or in the future.

I hope that ignorance is being dispelled by this book. I chose not to draw many illustrations from the outside, but to deliberately concentrate on expounding the Bible's teaching, convinced as I am that this is the best source of knowledge and great blessing.

Such a study of angels is going to stand us in

good stead for eternity. Here on earth, we get caught up in transitory things. Our clothes wear out and have to be discarded. The washing machine breaks down or the car wears out, and they have to be replaced. Even books and information learned in school soon become outdated.

That's not the way it is when it comes to the angels. Angels are not short-term missionaries in God's eternal program. The time will never come when He will turn to them and say, "Sorry, I have no further use for you." Angels will most certainly continue their work of praising God and worshiping Him throughout eternity. They will always be standing by to serve God in any way He desires.

You Will See

Are you looking forward to seeing angels in heaven? I am! The Bible sometimes describes angels as being like lightning, or like the sun, or as having eyes like burning lamps. I want to see them in person and find out through my own observation, and I believe we'll be able to do that.

Meeting angels in heaven will, I believe, be one of our greatest sources of joy up there. I think we will know angels just as we presently know people. You see, I believe there will be no strangers in heaven. We won't have to walk up to someone, shake hands, and then ask, "Who are you? Where did you come from?" No, in heaven we will have perfect knowledge, and we will know people and angels instinctively.

Ask Adam

Our heavenly knowledge of others is going to open up tremendous experiences that will delight our hearts. For example, imagine seeing Adam in conversation with the cherubim God detailed for guard duty in the Garden of Eden (see Gen. 3:24). They will be friends up there, and so will we.

What will Adam and the angels talk about? Well, perhaps Adam will have some things he wants cleared up concerning the Tree of Life. Perhaps Adam will say, "Angels, if you hadn't been there with that flaming sword, I would have sneaked back in and eaten some of the fruit."

"I know," an angel may respond, "but that would have been a terrible thing for you and all who came after you, for you would have lived forever in your sinful state. God is so merciful and gracious that He couldn't allow that. He had a much better plan of salvation."

Do you think I am overdrawing what may happen? Perhaps you even wonder if Adam got to heaven. I like to think he did. Although he sinned in eating of the tree prohibited to him by God, I just can't believe he continued in his rebellion. I feel sure he got back into fellowship with God, that he walked with God, talked with Him, and offered sacrifices for his sins. I look forward to meeting Adam and finding out from him what it was like to be the first of the human race.

Jacob in the Corner

How magnificent it will be to talk with Jacob in some quiet place about the angel who wrestled with him during the night. I would like him to explain to me the details of that amazing struggle between a man of great strength and an angel of superhuman strength. "Jacob, did you expect the fight to go on as long as it did? Did you realize that would be a turning point in your life and result in a change of names?"

Perhaps you would rather ask Jacob about his vision of angels going up and down from heaven, as the Bible relates in the account of his vision (see Gen. 28). I'm sure he would be glad to elaborate. Maybe Jacob himself will want to turn to the angels involved in case he wishes some clarification.

Other Opportunities

One reason heaven is going to be heaven and eternity is going to be so wonderful is that we can discuss such tremendous things as long as we wish. I, for example, want to sit and talk with godly people who lived at the time of the Tower of Babel. What did they think on that day when God came down and confused human languages so that it would be impossible for the building task to continue? And maybe I'll have other questions after rereading the story in Genesis 11.

I want to converse with the people who were there in the Israelite camp when Moses was up on the mountain receiving the Ten Commandments. I want to ask what in the world they could have been thinking when they had Aaron make a golden calf for them to fall down before and worship. How did they feel when Moses returned to rebuke them (see Ex. 32)? As you read the Scriptures, you probably come across many subjects on which you'd like more light. Well, in heaven, I think you will get it.

One After Another

On previous pages of this book, I have written about the role of angels in the lives of Joshua, Daniel, and the Three Hebrew Children. I will not take space here to go over those great happenings again, but perhaps in heaven you and I will be able to sit down with those famous personalities and receive from them more complete accounts than those given in Scripture. I don't think they will ever tire of telling the stories

they lived, for in doing so they will bring glory
to God.

Questions, Questions, Questions

Many things we will want to ask the angels
directly. How did they feel when Jesus took on
a human body and for a while was made lower
than the angels (see Heb. 2:9)? And what were
their emotions when Jesus returned to heaven,
His work on earth accomplished?

I wonder why angels are always referred to
in the masculine gender? Why are they considered not so much a race as "an innumerable company" (Heb. 12:22)? At times, angels have manifested themselves in human form as we have
seen. Do all angels have the power to do that? I
think we will find out in heaven.

What kinds of questions would you like to ask
the angels? Perhaps you will be eager to find
out why only Michael and Gabriel are named
for us in the Bible, and just how extensive is
Michael's authority as the archangel.

I think it will be interesting to inquire about
how angels reacted on appearing to men. We
know some men were afraid, some were awed,
and some fell down to worship. But how did the
angels feel about those reactions?

We know some angels have wings and some
apparently don't. Why? In what other ways do
they move about?

What did the good angels think when they witnessed the rebellion of Satan and watched as perhaps one-third of their number left heaven with him? Did they try to keep those foolish angels from taking that tragic step? Did they suspect something like that might happen when Lucifer began to boast about his beauty and position?

What did the angels feel when they watched the Lord Jesus being taken captive in the garden the night before His death, knowing that God's Son had but to speak a word and legions of their number would hurry to His aid?

Clarifying the Word

Something God said about angels has always fascinated me. God asked Job, "Where wast thou when I laid the foundations of the earth? Declare, if thou hast understanding.... when the morning stars sang together, and all the sons of God shouted for joy" (Job 38:4,7). "The morning stars" and "the sons of God" are terms used to describe angels. So we know angels were present at the creation of the physical universe. How did they feel about observing that tremendous act of our God? I'd like to ask them; wouldn't you?

Then, there are eight little words Paul wrote almost as an aside when he was considering the matter of Corinthian Christians going to court before secular judges to resolve misunderstandings. Paul wrote, "Know ye not that we shall judge angels?" (1 Cor. 6:3). I believe that will take place in heaven, but why will we judge angels? When? By what standards? What will be the results of our judgment? How is it that God has seen fit to give us that responsibility? What do angels feel about it?

There are so very many facts about angels that we still don't know. In heaven we will surely have our questions answered, and I think we will be simply amazed at all we learn about those fantastic beings God has created.

What of the here and now? I hope I have been able on the preceding pages to demonstrate in some measure the reality and ministry of angels to God's people, you, today. As you make your pilgrim journey from this world to the next, let them reach out to you, touch you at your point of greatest need, and fill you with all the joy of heaven.